REBELLION

Some Other Titles From New Falcon Publications

Aha! The Sevenfold Mystery of the Ineffable Love	–Aleister Crowley
An Insider's Guide to Robert Anton Wilson	–Eric Wagner
Bio-Etheric Healing	–Trudy Lanitis

Undoing Yourself With Energized Meditation and Other Devices
Secrets of Western Tantra: The Sexuality of the Middle Path
Dogma Daze —Christopher S. Hyatt, Ph.D.
Rebels & Devils; The Psychology of Liberation–Edited by **Christopher S. Hyatt, Ph.D.**
Aleister Crowley's Illustrated Goetia, Sex Magic, Tantra & Tarot:
The Way of the Secret Lover, Taboo: Sex, Religion & Magick
                                Christopher S. Hyatt, Ph.D., and DuQuette
Pacts With The Devil, Urban Voodoo: A Beginner's Guide to Afro-Caribbean Magic
                                –**Jason Black and Christopher S. Hyatt, Ph.D.**

The Psychopath's Bible	–**Christopher S. Hyatt, Ph.D., and Jack Willis**
Ask Baba Lon	–**Lon Milo DuQuette**

Aleister Crowley and the Treasure House of Images
    –**J.F.C. Fuller, Aleister Crowley, Lon Milo DuQuette and Nancy Wasserman**
Enochian Sex Magic and How To Workbook
            –**Aleister Crowley, Lon Milo DuQuette and Christopher S. Hyatt, Ph.D.**
Enochian World of Aleister Crowley   –**DuQuette and Aleister Crowley**
Info-Psychology, Neuropolitique, The Game of Life, What Does WoMan Want?
                                                –**Timothy Leary, Ph.D.**

Nonlocal Nature: The Eight Circuits of Consciousness	–**James A. Heffernan**
on What is	–**Ja Wallin**
Rebellion, Revolution and Religiousness	–**Osho**
Reichian Therapy: A Practical Guide for Home Use	–**Dr. Jack Willis**
Shaping Formless Fire, Seizing Power, Taking Power,	
The Magick in the Music and Other Essays	–**Stephen Mace**
The Illuminati Conspiracy: The Sapiens System	–**Donald Holmes, M.D.**
The Secret Inner Order Rituals of the Golden Dawn	–**Pat Zalewski**
The Why, Who, and What of Existence	**Vlad Korbel**

Steamo Goes to Havana, The Social Epidemic of Child Abuse
                                         Michael Miller, M.Ed., M.S., Ph.D.
Woman's Orgasm: A Guide to Sexual Satisfaction
            –**Benjamin Graber, M.D., and Georgia Kline-Graber, R.N.**

Other Titles by J. Marvin Spiegelman, Ph.D.

A Modern Jew in Search of Soul
Buddhism and Jungian Psychology
Catholicism and Jungian Psychology
Hinduism and Jungian Psychology
Mysticism, Psychology and Oedipus - A Small Gem
Protestanism and Jungian Psychology
Psychotherapy and Religion at the Millennium and Beyond
Psychotherapy as a Mutual Process
Reich, Jung, Regardie & Me - The Unhealed Healer
Rider, Haggard, Henry Miller & I - The Unpublished Writer
Sufism, Islam and Jungian Psychology
The Knight - A Small Gem
The Nymphomaniac
The Quest - Further Adventures in the Unconscious
The Tree of Life - Paths in Jungian Individuation
The Wisdom of J. Marvin Speigelman Vol. I - Selected Writings
The Wisdom of J. Marvin Speigelman Vol. II - Psychology and Religion

Other Titles by Dr. Israel Regardie
A Garden of Pomegranates
A Practical Guide to Geomantic Divination - A Small Gem
Attract and Use Healing Energy - A Small Gem
Be Yourself - A Guide to Relaxation and Health
Ceremonial Magic
Dr. Israel Regardie's Definitive Work on Aleister Crowley,
  The Eye In The Triangle
Healing Energy, Prayer and Relaxation
How To Make and Use Talismans - A Small Gem
Israel Regardie's The Foundations of Practical Magick
My Rosicrucian Adventure
Mysticism, Psychology and Oedipus - A Small Gem
Practical Magick - A Small Gem
Teachers of Fulfillment
The Art and Meaning of Magic - A Small Gem
The Body-Mind Connection, A Path to Well-Being - A Small Gem
The Complete Golden Dawn System of Magic
The Complete Golden Dawn System of Magic Book 1 - Ltd. Edition
The Complete Golden Dawn System of Magic Book 2 - Ltd. Edition
The Complete Golden Dawn System of Magic - The Black Edition
The Eye in the Triangle: An Interpretation of Aleister Crowley
The Golden Dawn Audio CDs, Vol. 1, Vol. 2, and Vol. 3
The Legend of Aleister Crowley
The Magic of Israel Regardie
The Middle Pillar
The Philosopher's Stone
The Portable Complete Golden Dawn System of Magic
The Tree of Life
The Wisdom of Israel Regardie - Vol. I
  Selected Introductions, Prefaces and Forewords
The Wisdom of Israel Regardie - Vol. II
  Selected Essays and Commentaries
The Wisdom of Israel Regardie - Vol. III
  Selected Articles, Introductions, Prefaces and Forewords
What You Should Know About the Golden Dawn
Wilhelm Reich, His Theory And Techniques
Aha! (Dr. Israel Regardie and Aleister Crowley)
Roll Away The Stone/The Herb Dangerous
  (Dr. Israel Regardie and Aleister Crowley)

MANY OF OUR TITLES AVAILABLE ON KINDLE!
Please visit our website at http://www.newfalcon.com

Copyright ©New Falcon Publications 2023

All rights reserved. No part of this book, in part or in whole, may be reproduced, transmitted, or utilized, in any form or by any means, electronic or mechanical, including photocopying, recording, or by any information storage and retrieval system, without permission in writing from the publisher, except for brief quotations in critical articles, books and reviews.

ISBN 13: 978-156184-516-3
ISBN 10: 1-56184-516-7

New Falcon Publications First Edition 2023

The paper used in this publication meets the minimum requirements of the American National Standard for Permanence of Paper for Printed Library Materials Z39.48-1984

Printed in USA

NEW FALCON PUBLICATIONS
2046 Hillhurst Avenue
Los Angeles, CA 90027
www.newfalcon.com
email: info@newfalcon.com

REBELLION

Introduction by Lon Milo DuQuette

Contributions by

William S. Burroughs • Timothy Leary, Ph.D.
Aleister Crowley • Israel Regardie • Jack Parsons
Richard Kaczynski, Ph.D. • James Wasserman
Lon Milo DuQuette • Osho Rajneesh
AND
Dr. William S. Hyatt, Ph.D.
Stephen Heller • Ad Veritatem

NEW FALCON PUBLICATIONS
LOS ANGELES, CALIFORNIA, U.S.A.

Acknowledgments

Our deepest appreciation goes out to the mage of the era, William S. Burroughs for his contributions to this book and for his life's work;

To the members of the JOT Pact who contributed to this project;

To Frater Superior Hymenaeus Beta of Ordo Templi Orientis for his permission to use the Crowley material, and for his valuable assistance with the Jack Parsons selection;

To Robert F. Williams, Jr., and Stephani Williams for the photographs of William S. Burroughs;

To James Wasserman for permission to use photographs from his book, *The Secrets of Masonic Washington*;

To Anderson Slade for the illustration on page 10;

To Harry Widoff/Bookateria.com for the photograph on page 102;

To Nancy Wasserman for her ruthless editing;

To authors, artists, photographers and models who made this work possible;

and

To Rebels everywhere!

Dedication

*To William S. Burroughs, Timothy Leary, Ph.D.,
Robert F. Williams, Jr. & Stephani Williams*

William S. Burroughs
*The foremost literary figure of our time,
author of **Naked Lunch** and many other works*

"He divines remedies against injuries; he knows how to turn serious accidents to his own advantage; whatever does not kill him makes him stronger."
Friedrich Nietzsche, *Ecce Homo*

Table of Contents

Introduction - *Lon Milo Duquette* — xiii

Part I
Prescription For Rebellion

Paradise Mislaid — 3
  William S. Burroughs

The Price of Freedom — 11
  James Wasserman

Goddesses, Guns and Guts — 23
  James Wasserman

Hymn to Lucifer — 37
  Aleister Crowley

Crowley's Rebellion — 39
  Ad Veritatem IX°

Living Thelema — 53
  Jack Parsons

Rebellion Is The Biggest "YES" Yet — 63
  Osho (Bhagwan Shree Rejneesh)

Table of Contents

Part II
The World of Chaos, Taboo and Transformation

Taboo And Transformation In The Words of Aleister Crowley
    Richard Kaczynski, Ph.D.   83

Undoing Yourself With Chaos Magic   95
    Robert F. Williams, Jr.

Devil Be My God   103
    Lon Milo DuQuette

The Black Art of Psychotherapy   107
    Dr. Jack S. Willis

The Cursing of Our Children   117
    From The Social Epidemic of Child Abuse
    Dr. William S. Hyatt, Ph.D.

Table of Contents

Part III
Reprogramming the Self

Twenty-Two Alternatives To Involuntary Death   127
    Timothy Leary, Ph.D. & Eric Gullichsen

Breaking Trance   139
    Steven Heller, Ph.D.

The Middle Pillar- *Chapter One*   143
    Dr. Israel Regardie

Introduction
Lon Milo DuQuette

*Unthinking respect for authority
is the greatest enemy of truth.*
   –Albert Einstein

Do what thou wilt shall be the whole of the law.

Rebel and Devils? An anthology of short works by some of the most controversial writers of the 20th century: William S. Burroughs, Robert Anton Wilson, Aleister Crowley, Timothy Leary, and a host of other radical minds of the day.

I had already worked on four book projects for New Falcon Publications including *Enochian World of Aleister Crowley, The Way of the Secret Lover, Aleister Crowley's Illustrated Goetia, and Taboo – Sex Religion and Magick.* How many publishers go out of the way to present ideas that are viewed by the majority of our neighbors as being obscene, subversive, blasphemous, insane, and dangerous? The market for such a work is very small. I joked that *Rebels and Devils* would hardly be a get rich scheme. I was flattered and a bit surprised when I was asked to contribute an article. I enthusiastically agreed. I had just the thing for the book.[1]

Compared with most of the other rebels and devils in this unique work my credentials might seem rather anemic. I was born in a pleasant suburb of Los Angeles in the late

---

[1] *See* Devil Be My God.

1940s, raised in a pleasant (but woefully unconscious) small town in Nebraska, and, until my sophomore year in high school, never seriously labored in my mind about politics, religion, the nature of consciousness or the meaning (or the meaningless) of life.

The war in Vietnam (and the very real possibility that I would be drafted to fight and perhaps die for something I really didn't understand) served to underscore the importance of being awake while my classmates quietly sleep-marched into body bags. I had no idea where to begin this waking up process, but I knew I would have to do something, and fast. As it turned out, it would be something I decided *not* to do that put me on the fateful road to rebel/devilhood.

I was pondering my predicament as I took my seat in the high school auditorium and prepared to endure a patriotic convocation sponsored by the American Legion, and featuring greedy recruiters from the various branches of the Armed Services there to hungrily harvest a fresh crop of cannon fodder. Naturally, the convocation began with a color guard of Boy Scouts trooping the American flag to center stage. As if we were now in the presence of the Holy Grail, the unseen voice of Principal Boyd serenely ordered the assembly to stand up and recite the "Pledge of Allegiance to the Flag of the United States of America."

Now, please understand that I had always been proud to be an American and loved the principles (as much as a high school sophomore understood them) of our republic, and all those "freedoms" that I knew were not enjoyed by citizens of many other countries around the world. But the Pledge of Allegiance to the *Flag* had disturbed me from the moment I was bullied into taking part in the exercise in elementary school. Today something snapped. Today I said to myself 'fuck no!' I remained seated and silent during the pledge. No one seemed to notice...but I was wrong.

Later in the day I was stopped in the hall by Mr. Brown, a new social studies teacher from Colorado who had just been hired to replace his recently deceased predecessor. He said he noticed that I had not stood for the Pledge of Allegiance and asked me why. I told him I thought the whole things was stupid and that I resented the whole assembly's attempt to suck my naive classmates into a stupid-sounding war. I fully expected to get a lecture on what a nasty, unpatriotic little bastard I was. Instead, I got a warm smile and an invitation to visit him at his apartment after school.

Over cigarettes and coffee I learned a history of Vietnam conflict that I'd never heard before–a history that the rest of the world seemed to already know. I learned that there was a bigger world out there. I learned that there were many Americans, including Senators and Congressmen, who felt that our involvement in the war was a very un-American thing to do.

In the months that followed I received a world-class education in radical politics. I gathered a small cadre of my misfit friends to join me in these afternoon sessions with Comrade Brown. I started to collect anti-war buttons and bumper stickers, took a short correspondence course in draft counseling, and the dawn of my Junior year was putting it to use teaching lunch hour sessions in how to legally and illegally avoid the draft. This naturally brought down upon me the scorn of the school administration. I was expelled twice–once for refusing to cut my hair, the second time for the outrageously inappropriate charge of "sedition." "Sedition!" For high school draft counseling! Only in Nebraska. A couple of letters from the local Episcopal minister friend in the ACLU got me back in class in short order, but I was branded a cowardly and unpatriotic communist traitor.

By my senior year I was a card carrying rebel. I joined the *Student Peace Union*, the *Young People's Socialist League*, and the *Students for a Democratic Society*. To all but a couple of girlfriends and a close circle of fellow travelers, Lon the rebel had now become Lon the devil and the most despised student in Columbus High School. I loved it.

When it came time for me to register myself for the draft, I appeared at the Selective Service office sporting a green beret with a large "Fuck the Draft" button pinned front and center. I also carried with me a letter dated 1950 from the California doctor who originally diagnosed my Perthes hip disease. It read, "Lonnie cannot exercise below the waist." I brutally intimidated the sweet little wheelchair-bound lady at the SS office threatening that if I weren't classified 4-F or I-Y, I would claim Conscientious Objector status and cause so much trouble there would be hundreds of boys in town who would want to do the same thing. It was a ridiculous threat, but since World War I no one in Columbus, Nebraska ever talked to the Draft Board like that.[2]

Then one afternoon in the spring of 1966 I was searching for cigarettes in the drawer of our living room hutch when I discovered a letter from the U.S. Department of Justice in Washington D.C. It was addressed to my mother and included the address and telephone number of the FBI field office in Omaha and the name of an agent for her to contact. Mom was at work so I confronted my father.

---

[2] I don't know if the threat worked because immediately upon graduation I moved to California. Mail from the Selective Service followed me for awhile, but I just ignored them and threw them all away unopened. Finally, the letters stopped coming. Could it have been that easy for everyone?

The poor man was already barrel-chested and weak from the emphysema. He moved to the couch and started to clean his pipe and nervously tried to talk with me between carefully planned breaths.

"Your mother's worried about you. She thinks you're getting in with some pretty dangerous people. Her cronies at work told her she was being silly but she went ahead and wrote to the FBI. That's the letter she got back. She's already called the Omaha office and told them everything she thinks she knows."

I asked if he had heard her conversation, and he said, "Only the part where she told them that you've fallen in with Communists and that they were teaching you to hate your mother."

We both laughed.

I still couldn't fathom what possessed her to do such a thing. I recalled only one occasion when my mother and I ever discussed politics. I drew her a picture of a bird with its wings spread to illustrate the various degrees of philosophies between the extreme left and the extreme right wings of American politics. It was a pleasant conversation (I thought) and pinpointed where FDR located on the wings and where Barry Goldwater and Lyndon Johnson were located on the big bird. I certainly didn't espouse any subversive or un-American sentiments. I guess the big bird just freaked her out.

Now she was freaking me out, because as innocent as my activities were, from the point of view of a wartime FBI investigation my activities might make me at least *appear* to be a person of interest.

I had taken a summer job delivering broken television sets to an Omaha electronics shop for repair. Each trip I had to wait there, sometimes up to five hours, before returning the 90 miles home with the repaired units. All that time in the big city enabled me to make contact with my urbane comrades in the peace movement, including several Episcopal priests and a Unitarian minister who introduced me to the aging former president of a large international labor union. This man, who had a son my age, was the most interesting character I had ever met. He was at the time an active member of the Progressive Labor Party, but for years was an organizer for the Communist Party U.S.A. He had pictures of himself with Cisco Houston and Woody Guthrie and Pete Seeger and the Weavers; he knew Gus Hall; he'd been shot in the back by strikebreakers in Dearborn, bitten by dogs in Selma, and jailed in Mississippi with Martin Luther King. I couldn't wait for Saturdays so I could visit this delightful page of walking history. I am sure if anybody was a target for domestic surveillance in those dark years it was my colorful commie mentor. But I was harmless enough. Nothing ever came from my involvement with the movement except a Washington dossier marked *Kids-so-wild-their-mothers-turn-em-in* or one for Mom labeled *Mothers-so-crazy-they-turn-in-their-kids*.

In the spring of 1966 I graduated from high school and instantly packed up and drove my blue 1960 VW van back to my Southern California birthplace and pretended to go to college. I registered at Orange Coast College of Costa Mesa. Officially, my major was Drama, but my real major was 'the 60s.' I immediately linked up with the local SDS whose off campus headquarters was a large two story old house in Costa Mesa.

Expecting to find the same kind of somber-faced, but work-shirted denizens of the new Left that populated the University of Nebraska, I instead was greeted by a cadre of some of the most beautiful young people that I had ever seen–surfer boys with sandy blonde locks, and the bra-less hippie goddesses with long straight hair and voices like Joan Baez. I was in teenage rebel heaven. I presented them with a homemade Viet Cong flag. They presented me with a pipe-load of hashish and an invitation to a lecture by the greatest (then) living rebel and devil of them all, Dr. Timothy Leary. My rebel/devil life was about to take a radical turn...inward. But this is another story for another time,[3] and I'm coming to the end of the space provided for me in this Introduction. I believe that it is safe to say that Dr. Leary's influence played a significant roll in shaping the lives, characters, attitudes, and ideas of the majority of the individuals who have contributed to this unique and historic publication.

In 1980, I and members of the OTO[4] Lodge in Newport Beach decided it was time that Dr. Leary received some kind of award–a token of appreciation for his influence upon the evolving consciousness of humanity. We named our award after one of the most infamous rebels and devils of them all, Adam Weisphaupt, the notorious founder of the Bavarian Illuminati. The plaque was laser etched on brass and mounted on heavy walnut. It was framed by the classic image of the Egyptian Goddess Nuit.

---

[3] Lon Milo DuQuette. *My Life With the Spirits*. (Boston, MA: Weiser Books, 1999).

[4] *Ordo Templi Orientis* (Order of the Temple of the East, or the Order of Oriental Templars) is an international fraternal and religious organization founded at the beginning of the 20th century. Originally it was intended to be modeled after and associated Freemasonry, but undner the leadership of Aleister Crowley was reorganized as a non-Masonic organization based on the Law of Thelema as its central religious principle. This Law-expressed as Do what thou wilt shall be the whole of the Law" and "Love is the law, love under will"–was established in 1904 with the dictation of *The Book of the Law*.

The inscription read:

> ## O.T.O.
> PEACE   TOLERANCE   TRUTH
> SALUTATION ON ALL POINT OF THE TRIANGLE
> Do what thou wilt shall be the whole of the Law.
> THE GUILD OF ADVANCED THOUGHT (G∴ O∴ A∴ T∴)
> HERU-RA-HA LODGE O.T.O.
> is honored to present to
> ## DR. TIMOTHY LEARY
> ### THE FIRST ANUAL
> ### ADAM WEISHAUPT ILLUMINATI AWARD
> In recognition of incalculable service to Humanity and others.
> Because of his inspired research and courageous example, Dr. Leary
> Is directly responsible for raising the consciousness of our planet.
> **"YOUR ONLY ALLEGIANCE IS TO LIFE"**
> Love is the law, love under will.
> Given this 11th day of July 1980 E.V.

After his death, this award was listed among the items sold by the auction house, Christie's in New York. If you are interested, you can still see a picture of it on Christie's website, Lot 13/Sale 8113.

In the years following, our lodge also presented the 'Illuminati Award' to two more rebels and devils whose work grace the pages of this book, Dr. Israel Regardie and Robert Anton Wilson. It is with a great deal of ironic amazement that I find my words bound between the covers of this remarkable book along with those of the late-great William S. Burroughs, Aleister Crowley, and Osho, and a new *dangerous* generation of Rebels and Devils.

Love is the law, love under will.

Lon Milo DuQuette
Costa Mesa, California, November 15, 2008

Part I

Prescription For Rebellion

William S. Burroughs
author of *Cities of the Red Nights,*
The Place of Dead Roads and *The Western Lands*

PARADISE MISLAID
William S. Burroughs

Paradise is a still picture. Paradise cannot change. The forbidden fruit is Time. And here are Adam and Eve...

She is eating sardines out of a can with a shoe-horn. She points to Adam with the horn:

"We're going to have to talk about our *relationship* and stuff."

God groans: "What have I done?"

Adam says, real stupid: "Huh?"

She adds, "Adam, we need to *emote*!"

Adam wears a dirty old t-shirt, the dirt so old it's gray. He stands in front of a cheap motel where they live in innocent bliss, surrounded by the Paradise Amusement Park. She hands him the *Big Apple*. He bites into it, and the apple turns into a candied apple. Carousel music. Shots from the shooting gallery. The Ferris wheel turns.

And here is an old clown, with a rusty scythe. A smell about him, sweet and evil and rotten. Not dangerous to a healthy adult, but Adam isn't healthy anymore. He is apple-rotten to the core.

Eve says: "Get out of here, and get me some money, too."

God echoes: "Get out of my Paradise. Get out and hustle, from here to eternity."

So they want me to do an endorsement for Peppy Jeans? What do they expect, a strip-tease?–at my age, in my condition?

"No," they assure me; "nothing that will offend the canons of good taste."

And then they write me as saying: "I was young once, with snakes dancing in my teeth."

Now, wait a minute. What you think I am, some snake-eating geek? And how did snakes get into this, anyhoo? and stuff...(oh, uh, yes I remember). A man has to draw the line *somewhere*.

Snakes in my teeth, indeedy;

I am not that fucking needy.

"So how is this?–'When I draw on my Peppy Jeans, I get a peppy feeling.'"

This will be a special-effects striptease, in which the jeans dance offa my ass and I chase them around the stage??

Now in evolution, the most basic thing is to find a niche– a niche that only you and yours occupy–and hold that niche, from here to eternity. It's the old Army game. If you lose the niche, you lose everything you can hold dear. And the worst thing that can happen to any species is *loss of habitat*: loss of the place in which it lives and breathes.

So how you find a niche? Look at yourself, and look around yourself. Here is a recent example: there was no niche for narcs until the Harrison Narcotics Act of 1914 slipped through–like Prohibition, when folks had other things on their mind. Before the Harrison Act, opium, cocaine, morphine could be bought across the counter in any American drugstore, from sea to shining sea. The law created a niche, and it was soon full to overflowing–and it keeps screaming for MORE MORE MORE: more personnel, more money.

Now how does one destroy such a cancerous factor? By destroying its habitat: the whole vast network of addicts, buys, stings, confiscations, stool pigeons, in which this creature lives and breathes.

Only things get Homo Sap up off his ass is a foot up it. If we don't stop this Reefer Madness, it will eat all our niches out from under us.

Time to streamline the medical profession. Future croakers will specialize in one operation, and know that inside out.

Diagnosis has become a separate specialty. They are known as "D's" and they tend to be of an elitist persuasion:

"Very few people are good at anything. You should see the diagnoses and test schedules passed along by hospitals. They have an insatiable appetite for tests. The more unnecessary the better, since they necessitate more tests."

The D walk in and sniffs: "Yellow fever. He stinks of raw meat."

"But that's impossible...he hasn't been..."

"What is his trade?"

"Uh, marine insurance."

"He goes on ships?"

"Uh, yes."

"So do mosquitoes."

"Supportive treatment. Prognosis unfavorable. Next case."

A psychiatric case returned for medical review:

"Disorientation...uh, drooling...Here are my tests so far."

"Liver?"

"Enlarged. Possible somatic symptoms. Subject's grandmother died of liver failure."

"The old bag drink?"

"I doubt it. She was one of those temperance ladies."

"Did you slur out 'drooling'?"

"Uh yes, it didn't seem important..."

"Wilson's disease...probably inherited. Treatment clearly indicated."

"Tests, doctor?"

"Look, when I do a D, I do a D–see? She's a classic Wilson. Does she have to slobber it all over you?"

The doctor snarls, and simpers, and sidles out of the room like a disgruntled crab, clutching his tests to his heart, hoping the D will be proven wrong. He isn't. In three months the Wilson is a normal healthy slut.

Next case. The D inhales deeply:

"What a lovely smell of new-mown hay...Typhoid. Get on it, in the name of Mary."

He turns to the patient: "Ate any good oysters lately?"

"The best. Portuguese oysters. They is known to be the best, like Portuguese Jews."

"Where?

"Joe's Seafood, at 49th and Third."

"Pass that address along to the Board of Health."

Next case: excruciating headache, chills and fever.

"That's enough. Malaria."

"Malaria in New York City? Didn't you say all cases are addicts?"

"Yes. It thrives in syringes."

"Nothing is true. Everything is permitted."

Last words of Hassan i Sabbah, the Old Man of the Mountain, Master of the Assassins. Interpreted by the ignorant as an invitation to unbridled license. On the contrary, realization involves exacting spiritual training. Everything is permitted *because* nothing is true. Everything is illusion.

"Do what you want is the whole of the law." Aleister Crowley's panacea. How many *know* what they want?

Everyman's ME is the dullest part about him. Who wants to hear about feelings of inadequacy? He'll be telling you about his bowel movements next, if you don't stop him. Just remember that in a case like this, deadly force is admissible. It's him or you.

W. Somerset Maugham thought that he had made the Devil's Bargain. If so, he was taken for a fool. The Devil's Bargain is always a fool's bargain, and especially for a writer. Since the Devil only deals in *quantitative* merchandise. He can make you a rich writer. He can make you famous. But he can't make you a great writer.

He always tries money first:

"Well, not much to spend it on–eh Gramps? Well now, how does a young body grab you?"

"Like a pea under a shell: 'Step right up. Hell under the shell.'"

To be young, you have to be *there* in Time. You have to *be* young, with the awkwardness, uncertainty and folly of youth. You have to be eighteen in time. And you are not eighteen. You are seventy-eight:

"Old fool sold his soul for a strap-on."

"Well, how about an *honorable* bargain? You could be a great research scientist and benefit mankind."

"There are no honorable bargains involving the exchange of qualitative merchandise, like souls and talent, for quantitative merchandise, like money and Time. So fuck off, Satan, and don't take me for dumber than I look."

Every man has the choice, at some moment in his life, to be God.

God put in this clause, and added: "Only a fool would take a job, when he learns that 'all-knowing' is all-feeling. A few hours in a cancer ward will usually cure a wise-ass.

God's Bargain and Satan's Bargain are both fool's bargains.

William S. Burroughs
Lawrence, Kansas
September 17, 1994

William S. Burroughs, born February 5, 1914, is the world-renowned author of *Naked Lunch, Queer, Interzones, Junky, The Soft Machine*, and *My Education: A Book of Dreams*, among many other works. He is a member of the American Academy and Institute for Arts and Letters and a *Commandeur de l'Ordre des Arts et des Lettres of France*. He is considered by many to be the foremost literary figure of our time. He died on August 2, 1997.

REBELLION

William S. Burroughs
author of **Queer, Interzones** and **Junky**
among many other works

Liber Anu vel DCXXXV
The Book of Hope
by Anderson Slade
©1995 Lion Serpent Publishing

THE PRICE OF FREEDOM
James Wasserman
Editor of the New Falcon Publications title: *AHA!*

Thrill with lissome lust of the light,
O man! My man!
Come careering out of the night
Of Pan! Io Pan!

I have come to realize, at age 46, that Liberty has been the entire basis of my life quest. I have used every technique I could find to maximize my Liberty–meditation, ritual magick, sex, drugs, sobriety, philosophy, personal economics, career orientation. I now believe that an understanding of political liberty is an essential part of my search for spiritual liberty.

Historically the gods of a conquered people become the devils of their conqueror's pantheon. Today's rebels and devils include those of us who still worship yesterday's gods of Individual Liberty and Inherent Individual Rights. Our would-be conquerors are the New World Order addicts, whose cradle-to-grave security and obedience models are inimical to individual Freedom. These power-junkies parade themselves endlessly upon the media stage, camouflaging their daily control-fix under the banner of Compassion, Global Interdependence, and Resource Management. Their addiction has caused them to both advocate and labor toward an abandonment of the Liberty unique to American society.

I too once embraced socialism as part of my learning process–until it became clear that a world bureaucracy run by social planners and civil-servants was one three-dimensional reality I truly had to fear. I now spurn the advance of the Age of the Expert, and the cultural madness in which the machine (designed by the international corporate mind-killers) becomes God. Thus, although I am a business owner, father, husband, law-abiding, tax-paying, U.S. citizen, my political views are those of a modern social pariah.

My spiritual path is identified with the teachings of Aleister Crowley and *The Book of the Law*. A logical corollary of this statement is that I believe in Divine Inspiration. I also believe that *The Book of the Law* was neither the first nor the last time divine inspiration penetrated human consciousness. Further, I believe the American Constitution and its Bill of Rights to be a divinely inspired model of a potential Thelemic society–as later articulated by Crowley in *Liber OZ* (a short tract, written in 1925, that expressed the political philosophy of *The Book of the Law* in words of one syllable). What makes the ideas of both *Liber OZ* and the Bill of Rights so radical is their guarantee of nearly unlimited personal liberty and individual right.

Implicit in seeking to maximize individual liberty is a recognition of the divinity inherent within each human being. Quoting *The Book of the Law*, "Every man and every woman is a star" and "...thou has no right but to do they will." These statements posit both a will to do, and an attainable celestial nature at the root of the self. The reigning political goal of a society built on these principles must be the encouragement of maximum individual liberty for the most unfettered growth of the divine inner potential. Simple enough–*if* you believe in the divine inner potential.

Respect for human nature is an absolute prerequisite to a vision of human freedom.

The U.S. Bill of Rights represents the first time in history that individual sovereignty was regarded as *primary,* and government sovereignty as *secondary.* The Declaration of Independence spells out America's founders' understanding of the *origin* of rights in no uncertain terms, "We hold these Truths to be self-evident, that all Men are...endowed by their Creator with certain unalienable Rights..." The inviolate supremacy of the *inalienable* rights acknowledged in the Bill of Rights is protected from the State. The "rights" acknowledged by the UN and other New World Order scams are *conditional* upon the will of the State. They are *contingent* rights, "given" or "dispensed" *by* the State. It is impossible to emphasize strongly enough the difference these two points of view.

The U.S. Constitution purposely sets up an *inefficient* government. This is no accident. Thomas Jefferson spoke of an American government "shackled by the chains of the Constitution." Imagine our New World Order addicts willingly cutting themselves off from their domination-fix.

In the Age of the Expert, the vision of an *inherently successful* humanity is considered a nineteenth century myth that today's "experts" have deemed inoperative. Social planners are heralded as the new deities who will bring order out of the chaos of an *inherently unsuccessful* humanity's unbridled and destructive passions–and channel these instincts into constructive byways. How they accomplish this modern miracle of course, may require the use of force. In simpler times, this would be called "Tyranny." Today, "Social Planning for an Orderly and Productive Society Under the Watchful Eye of the Corporate Oligarchy" might be a more long-winded, if politically correct means to describe the same thing. The ultimate end of this philosophy was conclusively forecast by George Orwell in *1984* and Aldous Huxley in *Brave New World*.

The hooded black figures with automatic weapons these days are no longer terrorists–they are government agents. To confirm this, let us invoke the shade of David Koresh and the eighty-some Branch Davidians who perished in the flames with him as the world watched TV. On February 28, 1993, one hundred federal police, armed with automatic weapons and badges showed up on private property, guns a' blazin'. Soon came hundreds more, with hundreds more guns and badges, adding tanks, Bradley Fighting Vehicles, loudspeakers, stadium lights, electronic surveillance equipment, and a mini army of professional cult busters and "expert deprogrammers." Next came hundreds of pages of newspaper and magazine articles, and hundreds of hours of TV and radio broadcasts, continuing the assault with their "objective" reporting–a barrage of character assassination and unsubstantiated rumor–painting this sect and its young leader as modern incarnations of the anti-Christ. Fifty-one days of torment and slander finally result in the greatest conflagration of modern "law-enforcement." In 45 minutes, the "fortress" of this heavily armed cult" burns to the ground like the pathetic tinderbox it was all along.

Our globally compassionate political leaders strut and fret their hour upon the stage, each one so willing to "take responsibility" you had to wonder when their jail terms would begin. Meanwhile, ACLU, Amnesty International, and other Establishment conscience-mongers are so silent you could hear a dead child's whimper. Editorial pages poke a few jabs at the BATF just to prove their independence, but the BATF isn't really as popular as the FBI anyway. The bottom line is, nobody cares. Koresh and the Davidians were weird, and had it coming.

Just ever so gradually, the house of cards begins to fall apart. Information surfaces to contradict the government/media disinformation, and many questions arise. Among a host of issues are the following:

1. The heavily armed cult appears to have owned about 200 rifles, or two per adult resident. Statewide in Texas, average gun ownership runs about four per adult.

2. Irrefutable evidence is provided that the loss of the element of surprise was known to ATF raid leaders before the raid. They shamelessly lied about this for months after the raid.

3. Three of the four dead ATF agents had been Clinton's bodyguards during the 1992 campaign. Unedited video feeds of the raid suggest these three may have been assassinated by another ATF agent, who tossed a grenade, then fired two unaimed machine gun bursts into the room they had just entered.

4. Neither Clinton nor Reno dare acknowledge that their much publicized desire to save the children was the primary cause of the children's death. The FBI turns out not to have been so sure of child abuse after all.

5. Highly respected attorneys who visited Mt. Carmel publicly accuse ATF of firing from helicopters through the ceiling of the women and children's living quarters. They swear the physical evidence supported Koresh's claims that agents fired first.

6. A sane assessment of tanks smashing into wooden walls–behind which bales of hay, kerosene lamps, diesel generators and propane tanks–casts doubts on claims by an FBI sniper to have observed black-clad masked Davidians setting fires. The sniper's statement is also known to contradict observations by newsmen during the first half hour of the live broadcast of the fire, before the disinformation squad could assemble.

7. A couple of government investigative experts are courageous enough to speak up and pin the tail on Reno, *et al*.

8. And finally a kangaroo court in February, 1994 exposes the extent of the government vendetta against the Branch Davidians. The judge overthrows the jury's innocent verdict with such arrogance that the jury foreman cries on the steps of the courthouse. And thereby undoubtedly sets the precedent for a successful appeal.

9. Multi-million dollar lawsuits against the government are filed both here and abroad.

10. And finally A&E Network offers a fairly unbiased hour-long report after nearly two years of an almost total media disinformation campaign.

A family in Idaho, the Weavers, gunned down by Federal agents in August, 1992 are also getting some acknowledgment, despite the earlier media blitz against their "white-supremacist," "armed extremist" profile. U.S. Marshals first shoot and kill the family's dog, and then shoot Weaver's 14-year-old son in the back, killing him. Next, 300 feds surround the Weaver cabin. And FBI agent blasts a .30 caliber hole in Mrs. Weaver's head, killing her as she cradles her ten-month-old baby in her arms. After 11 days, a severely wounded Weaver surrenders. He is later acquitted by a jury of his peers. In Weaver's case, he faces a human being for a judge, unlike his Davidian soul-mates. A secret Justice *(sic)* Department report leaked in December, 1994 acknowledges that Mrs. Weaver's constitutional rights were violated by the FBI's "rules of engagement" for that operation. (Strangely enough, these unconstitutional "rules" were written by one of the same public servants who incinerated the Branch Davidians eight months later.) While all the money or legal precedents in the world can't bring back a son or a wife, Rander Weaver is suing the government and will undoubtedly win. It's a good feeling to know that our government can rely on its taxpayers to cover its financial liabilities when it has been adjudged to have acted improperly.

We Americans are facing a daily information assault designed to persuade us to sacrifice our Liberty in the name of Collective Security. In late 1992, for the first time in history, more people were employed by various levels of local, state, and federal government than were employed by private industry. Those employed by government have only one purpose–to monitor us. We now have more people paid to monitor us, than we have people producing the money to pay our monitors.

The tyrants encroaching in our lives are dangerous because of their insatiable need for more control. In *Naked Lunch*, William S. Burroughs brilliantly describes the exponential grasping of addiction as the "Algebra of Need." Our political addict-experts have pounced into our very beds with their sexual speech codes, and will soon demand we make them responsible for licensing us to produce our children. Later they will insist on determining those children's schooling, profession, and place of residence (all in the name of global ecology, crime-prevention, human rights, etc., *ad nauseam*).

An enforced subservience of the individual to the "common good" is the current meaning of the word "Liberalism." In order to grasp the doublethink involved, read Jack Parson's collection of essays in *Freedom is a Two-Edged Sword*, published by New Falcon Publications. Written in the early 1950s, for Parsons, *Liberalism* meant what we would call today "Individualism," "Constitutionalism," even "Conservatism" (!) In any brainwashing procedure, one of the first patterns that must be broken down is the meaning of words. "Loyalty," "patriotism," "honor," must be gradually turned into the opposites to allow the naturally morally-directed psyche to maintain allegiance to its guiding principles, while acting in a conditioned manner–Orwell's classic FREEDOM IS SLAVERY.

Like any sane and decent person, I am concerned with war and political strife. My experience as a human being however teaches me that evolution and peace cannot be coerced, even in the name of the "greater good." And I become suspicious of people who want to coerce me. For example, even before the "fall" of the Soviet Union and the "liberation" of South

Africa, the United States boasted the largest percentage of its citizens in prison in the entire world. And now, the U.S. House and Senate, with cheer-leading from the White House, are attempting to outdo each other to prove how "tough on crime" they can really be. Build More Prisons. Makes sense. After all, since in 1990, 50% of new inmates in New York were imprisoned for the sale or possession of drugs, we need more prisons to make room for criminals as well as pot smokers.

However, I can't find a section of the Constitution or Bill of Rights that allows the Government to imprison people who are not committing crimes against others. In fact, the First Amendment guarantees free-expression; the Fourth Amendment guarantees privacy; and the Ninth and Tenth Amendments tell the Government exactly where it must stop. (Incidentally, there are bills in both the House and Senate to repeal the Second Amendment. And Comrade Clinton is still attempting to ram through legislation and rally public support to abrogate the Fourth Amendment, through warrantless searches in public housing.) If a person commits a crime while under the influence of drugs, he should certainly be imprisoned. If a person commits a crime with a gun, that person should also be severely punished. But the operative phrase is "If a *person* commits a crime"–not "drugs" or "guns."

In the final months of the Kennedy Administration, a 15 member Special Study Group was commissioned to evaluate the ramifications of a world at peace. The group met for two and a half years, after which they submitted their unanimous secret report to the Johnson Administration. One member anonymously leaked the report, which was published as *Report from Iron Mountain on the Possibility and Desirability of Peace*, with Introductory Material by Leonard C. Lewin, Dial Press, 1967.

Discussing the need to find a substitute, in a peaceful society, for the military function of providing an outlet for aggressive young people, as well as employment opportunities for the poor and under-educated, the report states, "Another possible surrogate for the control of potential enemies of society is the reintroduction, in some form consistent with modern technology and political processes, of slavery. Up to now, this has been suggested only in fiction, notably in the works of Wells, Huxley, Orwell, and others engaged in the imaginative anticipation of the sociology of the future. But the fantasies projected in Brave New World and 1984 have seemed less and less implausible over the years since their publication. The traditional association of slavery with ancient pre-industrial cultures should not blind us to its adaptability to advanced forms of social organization, nor should its equally traditional incompatibility with Western moral and economic values. It is entirely possible that the development of a sophisticated form of slavery may be an absolute prerequisite for social control for a world at peace."

The sinister perpetrators of the world government hypnotic hoax are powerful people in government, finance, and the media, whose self-importance allows them to feel they are better qualified to run our lives than we are. The really scary part is that we have given them the power to do so. Why? Because they *valued* it *more* than we did. We have been guilty of dereliction of duty. The price of freedom is eternal vigilance. And we have been asleep at the wheel. That personal, individual evasion of moral responsibility is the key to the slavery we are substituting daily for the American Constitutional Freedom that is the birthright of each member of this nation. Living with, and protecting, that terrible Freedom is the unique responsibility of everyone who dare call himself Initiate.

True compassion and true idealism demand that American society honor and defend its unique philosophical underpinnings. We can share this model with the entire world by example, functioning as a beacon of light and hope that all may see. The pathetic, guilt-ridden, hand-wringing and cringing proposed by the New World Order crowd are merely sophisticated psychological tactics to induce subservience. Today, self-aware, independent thinkers can "Just Say No!" to the Globaloney bullshit.

James Wasserman has been studying and practicing the Magical system of Aleister Crowley for over twenty years. He is also a noted author and a strong proponent of freedom and human rights.

GODDESSES, GUNS AND GUTS
James Wasserman
Author of *The Slaves Shall Serve: Meditations on Liberty*

> *Freedom is a need of the soul, and nothing else. It is in striving toward God, that the soul strives continually after a condition of freedom. God alone is the inciter and guarantor of freedom... Political freedom, as the Western world has known it, it only a political reading of the Bible.*
> —Whittaker Chambers, Witness

Soon after the success of the Cuban revolution in 1959, a group of soldiers entered the classroom. They spread themselves out, machine guns hung from their shoulders. Their leader addressed the assembled seven- and eight-year-olds. "Children, we want you to understand something about the revolution. Lay your heads on your desks and close your eyes. Make a prayer to God that when you open your eyes, you will have a container of ice cream sitting in front of you." A long pause followed as the children prayed in the hot room. "Now, open your eyes. There is no ice cream. That is the value of praying to God." Another pause. "This time, close your eyes, lay your heads on your desks and pray to Fidel for the ice cream." The adult who told me this story had been a little cagier than most of his classmates. He peeked out from between his folded arms and watched the soldiers swiftly placing containers of ice cream on each child's desk. The leader commanded the children in an enthusiastic tone, "Now, open your eyes." The children were, of course, delighted.

As I write, a courageous judge in Alabama has failed to prevent the removal of a monument, on which the Ten Commandments are inscribed, from in front of his courthouse. The ACLU, Southern Poverty Law Center, and other militant atheist lobby groups–fresh from their presumptive in victory in removing "under God" from the Pledge of Allegiance–arrayed against him and the Ten Commandments in full battle dress. "[I]ts view of God, its knowledge of God, its experience of God, is what alone give character to a society or a nation without God. But history is cluttered with the wreckage of nations that became indifferent to God, and died."[1]

George Mason's 1776 Virginia Declaration of Rights was a primary influence on Thomas Jefferson's opening paragraphs of the Declaration of Independence. Mason's refusal to sign the Constitution forced those who supported its ratification to promise to add the Bill of Rights, also based on the Virginia Declaration, to encourage others to vote in their favor. The First Amendment, states in part. "Congress shall make no law respecting an establishment of religion, or prohibiting the free exercise thereof..."

It is noteworthy that the misconstrued language of the First Amendment has become the weapon of choice of the atheist lobby to prevent people from freely exercising their religions. Like furtive smokers in New York City, those addicted to the vice of religion must confine their practice to the isolation of churches and homes, lest they contaminate a secular society with second-hand faith. Mason would have been amazed. Consider what he wrote in the last section of the Virginia Declaration of Rights.

---

[1] *Witness*, Whittaker Chambers, Random House, NY, 1952, pp. 16-17.

Section 16. That religion, or the duty which we owe to our Creator, and the manner of discharging it, can be directed only by reason and conviction, not by force or violence; and therefore all men are equally entitled to the free exercise of religion, according to the dictates of conscience; and that it is the mutual duty of all to practice Christian forbearance, love, and charity toward each other.[2]

Commenting on the language and context of the First Amendment (what is called "original intent), journalist and author David Limbaugh writes, "The Establishment Clause of the First Amendment prohibits Congress from establishing a national church. It also prohibits Congress from interfering with the right of individual states to establish their own churches if they choose (between seven and nine colonies had established churches at the time of the founding)– not that any would consider it today."[3]

One can imagine poor old Madelyn Murray O'Hare (the original atheist campaigner against prayer in school) rolling over in her grave.) Although since she didn't believe in the soul's survival of bodily death...well, you can see he problem.)

Here is the point I would like to make, stated in the simplest and most direct language:

---

[2] US National Archives & Records Administration http://www.archives.gov/exhibit_hall/charters_of_freedom/bill_of_rights/virginia_declaration_of_rights.html.
[3] David Limbaugh, "A Closer Look at Justice Moore, the Ten Commandments, and the Rule of Law." Posted August 27, 2003 at http://www/humaneventsonline.com/article.php?id=1649.

Without a belief in a Higher Power to whom one is directly and personally responsible, it is impossible to live as a free man or woman.[4]

One might question why someone who thinks as I do would subscribe to a belief system that states in its political program, "There is no god but man." (see *The Rights of Man* by Aleister Crowley). While the definition of both "god" and

---

[4] If the Younger Brethren will unclench their fists and revive from their swoons long enough to remember the concept of aspiration to the HGA, all will be well. Those secularists who honestly believe they live up to the standards discussed on page 73 may substitute "Moral Code."

"man" are well beyond the scope of this essay, it is possible to understand the term "man" as applying to a being far more exalted than a semi-rational evolved ape. Modern psychology widely accepts the existence of an unconscious mind. I hold the opinion that human beings also possess what might be called a "super-conscious" mind, and therein lies the truth of the statement, "There is no god but man."

I also accept that the alternative to the ethically aware, faith-based political and social order I am supporting here, is the UN, globalist, secular society being shoved down America's throat at an increasingly breakneck pace. In this world view, the "realist" or the "expert" has concluded that most people are not capable of governing their own lives, so they–the more self-disciplined leaders–must fill the vacuum by providing adequate controls on their moral, spiritual, and intellectual inferiors.

The human race requires discipline for its survival. At the most basic and personal level, without the discipline provided by our bone structure, we would collapse into shapeless blobs. On a more complex level, without the right ordering of human desires, society will collapse into a morass of anarchy and violence so often observed in times of crisis.

Political systems are necessary based on discipline. Laws and social customs reward desirable behavior and punish undesirable behavior. This is far from prudery or schoolmarmism. It is evolution. Think of the areas of life in which people face the most danger. The military and the medical professions both come to mind. They are two of the most hierarchically observant groups in society, utilizing the most stylized and ritualistically prescribed and proscribed rules of behavior. Those behavioral boundaries constitute a successful adaptation to the needs of their environments.

Anyone who has raised children is only too familiar with the consequences of behavior based solely on unbridled human desires. How many children have died or been injured by drowning, being hit by a car, or by electrocution, when indulging in their own unchallenged instincts? Parents are also well-positioned to observe the natural, biological self-centered point of view of the normal child. The human socialization process involves, at its core level, the learning of proper regard for the rights of others. This culturally transmitted instruction is no less holy or unnatural because it involves tutelage. The passing on and assimilation of knowledge and codes of behavior is fully compatible with the natural dignity of our species.

Tyranny is merely a form of discipline designed to bring about the right ordering of society–in this case by external compulsion. It is not illogical in the least. The collectivist Plato even considered it the greatest good in *The Republic*. Caroll Quigley, one of Bill Clinton's mentors and author of *Tragedy and Hope*, was more straightforward than most about the need for political domination by the elite–but I don't necessarily consider him an "evil" man. I think that he and many of the New World Order crowd think they are doing the right thing by attempting to manage society. After all, look at the mess we're in.[5]

In a political system that seeks to maximize individual Liberty, there must still be enough discipline to meet the

---

[5] The most egregious dishonesty of which they are guilty is not publicly accepting their own responsibility of much of that mess. Without laboring the issue, almost every policy advanced by the U.S. Government in the last sixty years has been either created, supported, and/or administered by a member of the Council on Foreign Relations (CFR). Convinced Communist traitor and first Secretary-General of the UN Alger Hiss was a member, as were Presidents Dwight Eisenhower, John Kennedy, Richard Nixon, Gerald Ford, Jimmy Carter, George H.W. Bush and Bill Clinton.

needs of human survival. In the case of a free society, the requisite discipline will be self-discipline.

Self discipline involves many different facets, not the least of which is learning and acting upon the lessons of the past, delaying gratification through rationally reviewing the results of behavior, and analyzing the legitimacy of a contemplated action. At the lowest level, satisfying hunger by scooping out food from a hot receptacle is behavior soon superseded by waiting for the right moment and using the appropriate instrument. On a more complex level, the

sexual instinct is usually most enjoyable when unaccompanied by an unwanted pregnancy. Going further up the chain, dishonorable behavior, often extremely tempting, will lead to self-recrimination in any person with a well-developed conscience.[6]

But what is the moral code of a free person? In my own case, I base my most successful actions on what I believe is *right*. What I mean by "right" is that behavior by which I am prepared to be judged by a higher standard. I can call that higher standard God, and imagine It to be a white-bearded classical figure, or imagine a Hall of Judgment with forty-two Assessors awaiting Tahuti's proclamation of the results of Weighing of my Heart against the Feather of Maat. I can calculate the effect of my behavior on the precious relationship with That which I have learned to call my Holy Guardian Angel. But whatever symbol set I might use to represent the Divine, you can bet your next paycheck it will include a sense of Fear. Holy Awe is another term to connote the same sense. It is an awareness that all I am, or can be, is secondary to a Magnificence which I cannot begin to describe, and on which I am wholly dependent. Was it not King Solomon who said Fear of the Lord is the beginning of Wisdom?

57. Follow out these my words
58. Fear nothing.
    Fear nothing.
    Fear nothing.
59. For I am nothing, and me thou shalt fear.[7]

---

[6] Defining "honor" is not an easy task. "Elevation of character, nobleness of mind, scorn of meanness" are all suggested by *The Oxford English Dictionary*. "Conscious self control in service to an ideal that embodies one's highest aspirations" may begin to approach the meaning.

[7] Liber LXVI, *The Holy Book of Thelema, Equinox III, No. 9*, Samuel Weiser, York Beach, ME, 1983, pp. 90-91.

I can be trusted, within the limits of my own spiritual development, to be honest, truthful, law-abiding, dependable, responsible, tolerant, caregiving, loyal, respectful, generous, etc. Part of the reason for this is my belief that my actions are being recorded by a Power to whom I am ultimately answerable. However I am equally capable of being an irresponsible, dishonest, low-life, whose selfishness and callousness is matched only by an internal compulsion to dominate every situation with which I am faced.

It's the "one from column A, one from column B" dichotomy that every self-aware human being will acknowledge–if he or she has the courage to look into the mirror of the soul. "My adepts stand upright; their head above the heavens, their feet below the hells."[7]

There is a distinct advantage to choosing for one's method of discipline a self-imposed moral code dependent on a growing understanding of a higher Power, and one's personal mission in life or True Will. The reward is a self-monitored and evolving rule of behavior, rather than one enforced by a confused 19-year-old wielding a machine gun, in subservience to leaders neither he nor I have ever met, following orders with which one or both of us may disagree. The deaths of the David Koresh and eighty-one other members of his church, after all, rested first on the unproved assumption by a Treasury Department functionary that Koresh may have violated the $200 tax mandated for the legal conversion of semi-automatic weapons to fully-automatic status.

Some further comments on this matter of respect for Authority. In the last decade, America has witnessed two very different styles of political administrations in Washington

---

[7] Liber XC, *The Holy Books of Thelema.*

D.C., at least on the surface. The country is virtually evenly divided between those who supported Clinton and those who support Bush (assuming one supports either). What seems different from any time I remember is the visceral hatred may people feel for one or the other. The media calls this "polarization of the electorate."[8]

But even if I happened to "like" Clinton or Bush, I would have to recognize that each of them is an imperfect being like myself. All of us are having enough trouble running our own lives. We should all exercise the courtesy and humility to stay out of each other's way. This was once called "acting like a gentleman," or "minding one's own business." Neither one of these politicians, or for that matter anyone else in the world, has the right to tell me what to do.

On the other hand I might want to do something that contradicted my own conscience or sense of morality. I may be so sorely tempted that I feel a real sense of annoyance and rebellion at realizing that what I may want is the wrong thing to do. Whether I do it or not will be based on my progress on the Spiritual Path. But at least one thing is clear. I have complete respect for (if imperfect obedience to) the source of Authority that oversees my behavior and defines my sense of right and wrong. There is no compromise or ambivalence

---

[8] Written in 2004. Now as we await the 2008 election, the Bush dynastic days are drawing to their close, and the Clintons, it seems, must await Chelsea to regain their grip on the collective throats of America. However, at least the media has moved beyond any concerns about "polarization of the electorate." It has been near unanimous in its shameless embrace of its messiah, the sainted Barack Hussein Obama. Like Mary in the New Testament, the media kneel before him, untie their hair, and anoint his feet–soiled from the rigors of his pilgrimage through the Chicago political machine. Thus, felons, racists, terrorists, and leftists have all been sanctified by the cameras, microphones, and word-processors of his sycophants. Meanwhile, John McCain, jettisoned by those he once considered his base, has punished them with Governor Sarah Palin. Way to go Mac!

here. But a human being, whether wearing a government hat or badge or any other symbol of authority, will never command that level of my allegiance.

Simply put, I am an imperfect being who recognizes the need for self-discipline, and is willing to be guided along the path of right action by a Power I recognize as my superior. The real advantage of inner freedom is that you get to serve a Power you respect.

Because, whether we like it or not, we will all serve a Power greater than ourselves. Those secularists who find the concept of God to be so repulsive or antiquated that it is beneath their dignity, condemn themselves to serve the power of man–whether it will be on tyrant with his blue-helmeted 19-year-olds, and another with his ninja-clad, jackbooted storm troopers, or a cigar-sucking, communist megalomaniac whose machine-gun wielding soldiers will be trying to prove to us and our children that he is God.

A Further Note

In view of a conversation with a friend who describes himself as a secular humanist and an agnostic, I must add the following.

There are two types of humanist. Individualists believe the fundamental concern for humanist thought should be the well-being and sanctity of the individual. They believe a person "owns" his own mind and body, that property is inviolate, therefore one must not be forced to any action that infringes his will. (Of course, conversely, the individual must not initiate force or violence against another.) Statists or collectivists hold a contrasting viewpoint. They believe the guiding principle against which humanist thought should be weighed is the interest and well-being of the group (as defined by the government or the "experts") which supersedes any rights of the individual. Both individualists and statists believe their program will result in the "greatest good" for humanity.

Libertarian humanists (individualists) are those who focus on individual rights. Many of America's Founders could be called libertarian religious humanists. Communists and socialist humanists (statists or collectivists) follow the school of thought that runs from the disciples of Rousseau during the French Revolution, through Karl Marx, to the likes of today's Howard Dean or Hillary Clinton.

I am happy to count as a friend any person with a well-developed ethical sense who does not believe in God, if he or she is honest and self-disciplined enough to understand the difference between "enlightened self interest" and self-indulgence; and who regards the rights of the individual as the absolute basis for his humanist beliefs. One of my intellectual heroes is Ayn Rand, an atheist, whose devotion to the highest ethical standards was, I believe, unsurpassed by the religious luminaries whom I also regard with admiration and respect.

This essay originally appeared in *The Slaves Shall Serve: Meditations on Liberty,* 2004, Sekmet Books, available at www.studio31.com and Amazon.com. The footnote on page 32 was written on Halloween night, 2008, some four days before the presidential election. The accompanying photos by James Wasserman are from the *Secrets of Masonic Washington*, 2008, Destiny Books, where they appear in full color.

Aleister Crowley (in 1906)
The Father of Modern Western Magick
Born 1875, Died 1947

HYMN TO LUCIFER
Aleister Crowley

Ware, nor of good nor ill, what aim hath act?
    Without its climax, death, what savour hath
Life? an impeccable machine, exact
    He paces an inane and pointless path
To glut brute appetites, his sole content
    How tedious where he fit to comprehend
Himself! More, this our noble element
    Of fire in nature, love in spirit, unkenned
Life hath no spring, no axle, and no end.

His body a blood-ruby radiant
    With noble passion, sun-souled Lucifer
Swept through the dawn colossal, swift aslant
    On Eden's imbecile perimeter.
He blessed nonentity with every curse
    And spiced with sorrow the dull soul of sense,
Breathed life into the sterile universe,
    With Love and Knowledge drove out innocence
The Key of Joy is disobedience.

Aleister Crowley
Also known as
*The Beast 666, The Wickedest Man Alive
and The Prophet of the New Aeon*

CROWLEY'S REBELLION

Ad veritatem IX°
Aleister Crowley is the author of these titles

The Enochian World of Aleister Crowley: Enochian Sex Magick
Aleister Crowley's Illustrated Goetia: Sexual Evocation
Aleister Crowley and the Practice of the Magical Diary
The Revival of Magick and Other Essays
The Pathworkings of Aleister Crowley
The Temple of Solomon the King
Little Essays Toward Truth
The Equinox of the Gods
Gems From the Equinox
The Heart of the Master
Eight Lectures on Yoga
Magick Without Tears
The World's Tragedy
The Law Is For All
AHA!

Do what thou wilt shall be the whole of the Law.

Aleister Crowley will be remembered as one of the most famous Rebels and Devils of all time. His proclamation of the Law of Thelema re-oriented the fundamental philosophical and religious foundations of Western society. And in recent years, O.T.O. (the first of the Orders of Antiquity to embrace the Law of Thelema) has helped extend the teachings of *The Book of the Law* to lands and cultures as distant as Japan.

In preparing this essay for publication, we have decided to let Crowley speak for himself, quoting his

New Comment to *The Book of the Law*, 1925, copyright O.T.O., published in an abridged edition by New Falcon Publications as The Law Is For All, edited by Israel Regardie. Chapter and verse citations, as well as page numbers, of the extracts are provided for ease of reference.

The reader may decide whether these thought, penned some seventy years ago, remain as the very vanguard of modern concerns as we prepare to enter the 21st Century.

On The Nature Of Man & God

Every man and every woman is not only a part of God, but the Ultimate God. "The Centre is everywhere and the circumference nowhere". The old definition of God takes new meaning for us. Each one of us is the One God... [p. 75]

Each man instinctively feels that he is the Centre of the Cosmos, and philosophers have jeered at his presumption. But it was he that was precisely right. The yokel is no more 'petty' than the King, nor the earth than the Sun. Each simple elemental Self is supreme, Very God of Very God. Ay, in this Book is Truth almost insufferably splendid, for Man has veiled himself too long from his own glory; he fears the abyss, the ageless Absolute. But Truth shall make him free! [I, 4, p. 76]

We are not to regard ourselves as base beings, without whose sphere is Light or "God". Our minds and bodies are veils of the Light within. The uninitiate is a "dark star", and the Great Work for him is to make his veils transparent by 'purifying' them. This 'purification' is really 'simplification'; it is not that the veil is dirty, but that the complexity of its folds makes it opaque. The Great Work therefore consists principally in the solution of complexes. Everything in itself is perfect, but when things are muddled, they become 'evil'... The Doctrine is evidently of supreme importance, from its position as the first 'revelation' of Aiwass. [I, 8, p. 81-82]

The type of tailless simian who finds himself a mere forked radish in a universe of giants clamouring for hors d'oeuvres must take refuge from Reality in Freudian phantasies of 'God'. He winces at the touch of Truth; and shivers at his nakedness in Nature.

He therefore invents a cult of fear and shame, and makes it presumption and blasphemy to possess courage and self-respect. He burrows in the slime of "reverence, and godly fear" and makes himself houses of his own excrement, like the earthworm he is. He shams dead, like other vile insects, at the approach of danger; he tries to escape notice by assuming the colour and form of his surroundings, using 'protective mimicry' like certain other invertebrates.

He exudes stink or ink like the skunk or the cuttle-fish, calling the one morality and the other decency. He is slippery with hypocrisy, like a slug; and, labeling the totality of his defects perfection, defines God as feces so that he may flatter himself with the epithet divine. The whole manoeuvre is described as religion. [II, 77-78, p. 261-262]

Political Liberty

The Book of the Law flings forth no theological fulminations; but we have quarrels enough on our hands. We have to fight for Freedom against oppressors, religious, social, or industrial; and we are utterly opposed to compromise. Every fight is to be a fight to the finish; each one of us for himself, to do his own will; and all of us for all, to establish the Law of Liberty...

Let every man bear arms, swift to resent oppression, generous and ardent to draw sword in any cause, if justice or freedom summon him! [III, 57, p. 317]

As the practical ethical of the Law, I have formulated in words of one syllable my declaration of the

Rights of Man

Do what thou wilt shall be the whole of the Law.

There is no god but Man.

Man has the right to live by his own Law.

Man has the right to live in the way that he wills to do.

Man has the right to dwell where he wills to dwell.

Man has the right to move as he will on the face of the Earth.

Man has the right to eat what he will.

Man has the right to drink what he will.

Man has the right to think as he will.

Man has the right to speak as he will.

Man has the right to write as he will.

Man has the right to mould as he will.

Man has the right to paint as he will.

Man has the right to carve as he will.

Man has the right to work as he will.

Man has the right to rest as he will.

Man has the right to love as he will, when, where and whom he will.

Man has the right to die when and how he will.

Man has the right to kill those who would thwart these rights.

[III, 60, p. 321]

[Ed. Note: In a letter to Gerald Yorke, dated 9/13/41, Crowley wrote, "Rights of Man is an historical document. The items don't go easily on the Tree; but I've got them down to give sections: moral, bodily, mental, sexual freedom, and the safeguard tyrannicide..."–quoted in *Magick*, Weiser, 1994, ed. Hymenaeus Beta]

Social Values

This thesis concerning compassion is the most palmary importance in the ethics of Thelema. It is necessary that we stop, once for all, this ignorant meddling with other people's business. Each individual must be left free to follow his own path! America is peculiarly instance on these points. Her people are desperately anxious to make the Cingalese wear furs, and the Tibetans vote, and the whole world chew gum, utterly dense to the fact that most other nations, especially the French and British, regard 'American institutions' as the lowest savagery, and forgetful or ignorant of the circumstances that the original brand of American freedom—which really was Freedom—contained the precept to leave other people severely alone, and thus assured the possibility of expansion on his own lines to every man. [I, 13-31, p. 89-90]

There is a good deal of the Nietzschean standpoint in this verse. It is the evolutionary and natural view. Of what use is it to perpetuate the misery of Tuberculosis, and such diseases, as we now do? Nature's way is to weed out the weak. This is the most merciful way, too. At present all the strong are being damaged, and their progress hindered by the dead weight of the weak limbs, the diseased limbs and the atrophied limbs. The Christians to the Lions!

Our humanitarianism, which is the syphilis of the mind, acts on the basis of the lie that the King must die. The King is beyond death; it is merely a pool where he dips for refreshment. We must therefore go back to Spartan ideas of education; and the worst enemies of humanity are those who wish, under the pretext of compassion, to continue its ills through the generations. The Christians to the Lions!

Let weak and wry productions go back into the melting-pot, as is done with flawed steel castings. Death will purge, reincarnation make whole, these errors and abortions. Nature herself may be trusted to do this, if only we will leave her alone. But what of those who, physically fitted to live, are tainted with rottenness of soul, cancerous with the sin-complex? For the third time I answer: The Christians to the Lions! [II, 21, p. 176-177]

It has naturally been objected by economists that our Law, in declaring every man and every woman to be a star, reduces society to its elements, and makes hierarchy or even democracy impossible. The view is superficial. Each star has a function in its galaxy proper to its own nature.

Much mischief has come from our ignorance in insisting, on the contrary, that each citizen is fit for any and every social duty. But also our Law teaches that a star often veils itself from its nature. Thus the vast bulk of humanity is obsessed by an abject fear of freedom; the principal objections hitherto urged against my Law have been those of people who cannot bear to imagine the horrors which would result if they were free to do their own wills. [II, 58, p. 207]

Personal Values

Each star is unique, and each orbit apart; indeed, that is the corner-stone of my teaching, to have no standard goals or standard ways, no orthodoxies and no codes. The stars are not herded and penned and shorn and made into mutton like so many voters! I decline to be bell weather, who am born a Lion! I will not be collie, who am quicker to bite than to bark, I refuse the office of shepherd, who bear not a crook but a club. [I, 35-37 p. 93]

All strength and all skill should be flung with a spendthrift gesture on the counter of the merchant of madness. On the steel of your helmet let there be gold inlaid with the motto "Excess." [I, 52, p. 126]

It is bad Magick to admit that one is other than One's inmost self. One should plunge passionately into every possible experience; by doing so one is purged of those personal prejudices which we took so stupidly for ourselves, though they prevented us from realizing our true Wills and from knowing our Names and Natures. The Aspirant must well understand that it is no paradox to say that the Annihilation of the Ego in the Abyss is the condition of emancipating the true Self, and exalting it to unimaginable heights. So long as one remains "one's self." One is overwhelmed by the Universe; destroy the sense of self, and every event is equally an expression of one's Will, since its occurrence is the resultant of the concourse of the forces which one recognizes as one's own. [II, 8, p. 166]

The Secret of Magick is to "enflame oneself in praying." This is the ready test of a Star, that it whirls flaming through the sky. You cannot mistake it for an Old Maid objecting to Everything. This Universe is a wild revel of atoms, men, and stars, each one a Soul of Light and Mirth, horsed on Eternity. [II, 34, p. 207]

Drugs

Drunkenness is a curse and a hindrance only to slaves. Shelly's couriers were 'drunk on the wind of their own speed.' Anyone who is doing his true Will is drunk with the delight of Life.

Wine and strange drugs do not harm people who are doing their will; they only poison people who are cancerous with Original Sin. In Latin countries where Sin is taken seriously, and sex-expression is simple, wholesome, and free, drunkenness is a rare accident. It is only in Puritan countries, where self-analysis, under the whip of a coarse bully like Billy Sunday, brings the hearer to 'conviction of sin,' that he hit first the 'trail' and then the 'booze.' Can you imagine an evangelist in Taormina? It is to laugh...

Truth is so terrible to these detestable mockeries of humanity that the thought of self is a realization of hell. Therefore they fly to drink and drugs as to an anaesthetic in the surgical operation of introspection.

The craving for these things is caused by the internal misery which their use reveals to the slave-souls. If you are really free, you can take cocaine as simply as salt-water taffy. There is no better rough test of a soul than its attitude to drugs. If a man is simple, fearless, eager, he is all right; he will not become a slave. If he is afraid, he is already a slave. Let the whole world take opium, hashish, and the rest; those who are liable to abuse them were better dead. [II, 22, p. 186]

Sexual Values

There shall be no property in human flesh. The sex instinct is one of the most deeply-seated expressions of the will; and it must not be restricted, either negatively by preventing its free function, or positively by insisting on its false function...

The sexual act is a sacrament of Will. To profane it is the great offense. All true expression of it is lawful; all suppression or distortion is contrary to the Law of Liberty. To use legal or financial constraint to compel either abstention or submission, is entirely horrible, unnatural and absurd. [I, 41, p. 98]

We of Thelema are not the slaves of Love. "Love under will" is the Law. We refuse to regard love as shameful and degrading, as a peril to body and soul. We refuse to accept it as the surrender of the divine to the animal; to us it is the means by which the animal may be made the Winged Sphinx which shall bear man aloft to the House of the Gods.

We are then particularly careful to deny that the object of love is the gross physiological object which happens to be Nature's excuse for it. Generation is a sacrament of the physical Rite, by which we create ourselves anew in our own image, weave in a new flesh-tapestry the Romance of our own Soul's History. But also Love is a sacrament of trans-substantiation whereby we initiate our own souls; it is the Wine of Intoxication as well as the Bread of Nourishment. "Nor is he for priest designed/Who partakes only in one kind." [p. 109]

"As ye will." It should be abundantly clear from the foregoing remarks that each individual has an absolute and indefeasible right to use his sexual vehicle in accordance with its own proper character, and that he is responsible only to himself. But he should not injure himself and his right aforesaid; acts invasive of another individual's equal rights are implicitly self-aggressions. A thief can hardly complain on theoretical grounds if he himself is robbed. Such acts as rape, and the assault or seduction of infants, may therefore be justly regarded as offenses against the Law of Liberty, and repressed in the interests of that Law. [p. 110]

Every one should discover, by experience of every kind, the extent and intention of his own sexual Universe. He must be taught that all roads are equally royal, and that the only question for him is "Which road is mine?" All details are equally likely to be of the essence of his personal plan, all equally 'right' in themselves, his own choice of the one as correct as, and independent of, his neighbour's preference for the other. [p. 111]

The Beast 666 ordains by His authority that every man, and every woman, and every intermediately-sexed individual, shall be absolutely free to interpret and communicate Self by means of any sexual practices soever, whether direct or indirect, rational or symbolic, physiologically, legally, ethically, or religiously approved or no, provided only that all parties to any act are fully aware of all implications, and responsibilities thereof, and heartily agree thereto. [I, 50-51, p. 114]

The act of Love, to the bourgeois, is a physical relief like defecation, and a moral relief from the strain of the drill of decency; a joyous relapse into the brute he has to pretend he despises. It is a drunkenness which drugs his shame of himself, yet leaves him deeper in disgust. It is an unclean gesture, hideous and grotesque. It is not his own act, but forced on him by a giant who holds him helpless; he is half madman, half automaton when he performs it. It is a gawky stumbling across a black foul bog, oozing a thousand dangers. It threatens him with death, disease, disaster in all manner of forms. He pays the coward's price of fear and loathing when pedlar Sex holds out his Rat-Poison in the lead-paper wrapping he takes for silver; he pays again with vomiting and with colic when he has gulped it in his greed. [p.135]

Therefore, the Love that is Law is not less Love in the petty personal sense; for Love that makes two One is the engine whereby even the final Two, Self and Not-Self, may become One, in the mystic marriage of the Bride, the Soul, with Him appointed from eternity to espouse her, yea, even the Most High, God All-in-All, the Truth.

Therefore we hold Love holy, our heart's religion, our mind's science. Shall He not have His ordered Rite, His priests and poets, His makers of beauty in colour and form to adorn Him, His makers of music to praise Him? Shall not His theologians, divining His nature, declare Him? Shall not even those who but sweep the courts of His temple, partake thereby of His person? And shall not our science lay hands on Him, measure Him, discover the depths, calculate the heights, and decipher the laws of His nature? [I, 52, p. 136]

Women's Rights

Laws against adultery are based upon the idea that woman is a chattel, so that to make love to a married woman is to deprive the husband of her services. It is the frankest and most crass statement of a slave-situation. To us, every woman is a star. She has therefore an absolute right to travel in her own orbit. There is no reason why she should not be the ideal hausfrau, if that chance to be her will. But society has not right to insist upon that standard. It was, for practical reason, almost necessary to set up such taboos in small communities, savage tribes, where the wife was nothing but a general servant, where the safety of the people depended upon a high birth-rate. But today woman is economically independent, becomes more so every year. The result is that she instantly asserts her right to have as many or as few men or babies as she wants or can get; and she defies the world to interfere with her. More power to her–elbow! [I, 41, p.99]

We of Thelema say that "Every man and every woman is a star." We do not fool and flatter women; we do not despise and abuse them. To us a woman is Herself, absolute, original, independent, free, self-justified, exactly as a man is.

We dare not thwart Her Going, Goddess she! We arrogate no right upon Her will; we claim not to deflect Her development, to dispose of Her desires, or to determine Her destiny. She is Her own sole arbiter; we ask no more than to supply our strength to Her, whose natural weakness else were prey to the world's pressure. Nay more, it were too zealous even to guard Her in Her Going; for She were best by Her own self-reliance to win Her own way forth!

We do not want Her as a slave; we want Her free and royal, whether Her love fight death in our arms by night, or Her loyalty ride by day beside us in the Charge of the Battle of Life.

"Let the woman be girt with a sword before me!"

"In her is all power given."

So sayeth this our *Book of the Law*. We respect Woman in the self of Her own nature; we do not arrogate the right to criticise her. We welcome her as our ally, come to our camp as her Will, free-flashing, sword-swinging, hath told Her, Welcome, thou Woman, we hail thee, Star shouting to Star! Welcome to rout and to revel! Welcome to fray and to feast! Welcome to vigil and victory! Welcome to war with its wounds! Welcome to peace with its pageants! Welcome to lust and to laughter! Welcome to board and to bed! Welcome to trumpet and triumph; welcome to dirge and to death!

It is we of Thelema who truly love and respect Woman, who hold her sinless and shameless even as we are; and those who say that we despise Her are those who shrink from the flash of our falchions as we strike from her limbs their foul fetters. [p. 307-308]

The Book of the Law is the Charter of Woman; the Word Thelema has opened the lock of Her "girdle of chastity." Your Sphinx of stone has come to life; to know, to will, to dare and to keep silence. [p. 308]

But now the Word of Me the Beast is this; not only art thou Woman, sworn to a purpose of not thine own; thou art thyself a star, and in thyself a purpose to thyself. Not only mother of men art thou, or whore to men; serf to their need of Life and Love, not sharing in their Light and Liberty; nay, thou art Mother and Whore for thine own pleasure; the Word I say to Man I say to thee no less; Do what thou wilt shall be the whole of the Law! [III, 55, p. 30]

Love is the law, love under will.

Jack Parsons
Rocket Man

LIVING THELEMA
Jack Parsons
Author of the New Falcon Publication title:
Freedom Is A Two-Edged Sword

I will attempt to present you with the outline of a practical reduction of the philosophy behind *The Book of the Law*, as it applies to our modern life.

This will be difficult, since there is an enormous background of technical, historical, social, and psychological data which I shall be forced to omit. This is all available. I hope that you will be sufficiently interested to review it yourself, if you have not done so.

If you will remember that I am dealing with the end product of this material, and trying, in a very short period, to condense this into a practical conclusion, I will appreciate your tolerance.

There are certain individuals who aspire to a maximum of independence in thought and in action, in order to achieve the optimum in the function of their nature and their creative will.

From among such have come the dreamers, and creators, the leaders and revolutionaries, artists and poets and scientists. All that we know of progress and of culture has come from them; all, out of the Neolithic swamp, by fire and air, by earth and water, and by the creative word, has come from those minds, and from those hands.

The anthropoid mind fears and mistrusts such sports, and rides an unwilling ape on the coattails of the creative evolute. Unwilling, unwitting, and often sometimes more than that.

In the indomitable will of the first order genius, there is sufficient ferocity and subtlety to overcome arboreal opposition, although the manifest result is usually post mortem, over a somewhat mutilated corpse.

But there are numberless fine minds, men and women of high talent and culture, who, lacking a little in the internal certainty, or facing an overwhelming social opposition, have deployed into futility and failure.

We propose a philosophy and a way of life having a pragmatic appeal to such minds.

A vast number of the human race has the mentality of slaves. Following Barnum, we can also deduce an appropriate number of slave masters.

There is no criticism here. The orders of nature are obvious, and acceptable to the philosophic. But, to the slave mind, there is often something unendurable in the notion of freedom and independence; it would have all men as its brothers in bondage. With this, the slave masters are in full accord.

It would be tedious to examine the techniques by which slavery has been fostered, the superstitious and authoritative devices, religious, political, social and economic, which have forged the chains. Whole philosophies, conceiving the universe of nature as sorrow, and the nature of man as sin, have been constructed to palliate sacrifice, expiation, and obedience.

God and Pope and king, society, humanity, the people, the proletariat, the family, war, the national emergency and all the other bogeys from the armory of fear have been summoned to confront the non-groveler. And those psychological weapons have been terribly enhanced.

This is obvious, and there is room in the world for animal acts and animal trainers—but not more than enough room!

If the individual abdicates his independence in the face of this rabbit hypothesis, this prestige suggestion, then he has deserved the bondage into which he is delivered.

It is a matter of balance. The leopard won't change his spots, not very rapidly, nor is it needful that he should. It is only needful that the Lion take his proper place in the jungle, and keep the leopard where he belongs, and the rabbit.

The creative individual must take his place as a creative leader in society. He must fulfill his destiny and his responsibility; he can achieve both in fearlessly following his creative will, his own inner truth, and, in inevitable corollary, he must and assist others who strive to do likewise.

Then, by leading the slaves a little out of slavery, and the masters a little into humanity, and culture, maintaining all the while his own inviolable independence, he will achieve that balance which alone gives significance to the human story.

Liber 77 Vel Oz
The Rights of Man

Do what thou wilt shall be the whole of the Law.
There is no god but Man.
Man has the right to live by his own Law.
Man has the right to live in the way that he wills to do.
Man has the right to dwell where he wills to dwell.
Man has the right to move as he will on the face of the Earth.
Man has the right to eat what he will.
Man has the right to drink what he will.
Man has the right to think as he will.
Man has the right to speak as he will.
Man has the right to write as he will.
Man has the right to mould as he will.
Man has the right to paint as he will.

Man has the right to carve as he will.
Man has the right to work as he will.
Man has the right to rest as he will.
Man has the right to love as he will, when, where and whom he will.
Man has the right to die when and how he will.
Man has the right to kill those who would thwart these rights.
Love is the law, love under will.

This exposition of the Rights of Man is a statement of first principles. You are referred to Crowley's works, the writings of Nietzsche, Mencken and Bertrand Russell; Emerson's essay on Self-Reliance; and the Declaration of Independence and Bill of Rights in the American Constitution. Here I am not unduly concerned with Theory, but rather with you, who, like myself, have independently reached these conclusions, and who are interested in a practical reduction.

Freedom is twofold; there is the freedom within, and the freedom without, and, like all things, the first freedom starts at the home plate.

The mainspring of an individual is his creative will. This will is the tone of his tendencies, his destiny, his inner truth. It is one with the force that makes the birds sing and flowers bloom; as inevitable as gravity, as implicit as a bowel movements, it informs alike atoms and men and suns.

The the man who knows this will, there is no why or why not; no can or cannot; he is!

There is no known force that can turn an apple into an alley cat; there is no known force that can turn a man from his will. This is the triumph of genius, that, surviving the centuries, enlightens the world.

This force burns in every man.

There are those who are too cowardly, too weak, to seek or express it.

There are those who are too full of pretense, of gullibility, of fear and greed to give it utterance.

Their lot is bitterness, failure and frustration; dust and ashes are their portion.

There are those who are bewildered, at odds with themselves, overwhelmed by adversity. They seek the light, and if they persevere, they will find it–within Themselves.

What are the obstacles to the attainment of the Will? There are many, but they may be grouped into certain primary divisions. And the name of every one of them is FEAR.

1. Fear of Incompetence: I would like to, but I could never do it. This is the flimsiest of excuses;–a narcissistic pap poisoning creation at its source. Confidence, enthusiasm, belief, egotism are the roots of creation.

BELIEVE IN YOURSELF; That is the first rule. Humility can come later. Build yourself to yourself–be proud–you are unique, and marvelously made. There is no other like you.

2. Fear of the opinion of others: What would people say? What people–what would they say? To Hell with them. Every genius that lighted the world has outraged public opinion–do you fear that pack of cards?

BE YOURSELF: Be true to yourself, be honest, enjoy yourself, go your own way, the way of the stars.

3. Fear of hurting others: Mother wouldn't want me to–! Are you yourself or another? Whose life do you live, to whom are you responsible, who is your master? Shall we ban cigarettes because they make Mrs. Grundy cough; hang lumber dealers because Christ was crucified, and rend Edison because Johnny was electrocuted?

Does it kill mother when you stay out until one? Is hubby so dreadfully hurt over that flirtation, and wifey in tears about the blonde? This is a subtle device of the slave master–"do what I say or I'" feel badly."

EXPRESS YOURSELF: Live your own life–follow your own star–as the Bible has it: "Forsake your father and mother"; "Let the dead bury the dead";–let the sick tend the sick–but follow yourself and no other christ or god. You are sufficient; you justify yourself; you are your own reason: THERE IS NO MORE NEEDED!

You should be polite about it; you may even be gentle about it. Wanton hurt is needless and gains nothing; but inner, inflexible strength, terribly gentle in its own right of expression, can and must follow its own Will as surely as a star follows its own orbit, undeterred and undisturbed by the wailing of inhabitants of minor satellites.

4. Fear of insecurity: I might lose my job. This is the most paltry, the most despicable of the excuses–this slavish whine for daily bread–anything you say, masters. I'll be good; just feed me!

HAVE FORTITUDE: Be courageous, and the adventure of Life is yours. Failure–can there be an ultimate failure where manhood is sustained? Is not any failure in freedom better than any success in the Slave Pen?

Yes, you might agree, (at least I assume that somebody might agree) but these things are difficult. Where do we start?

We start, naturally, with the least of the little things. For on the other end of the fulcrum from that little thing is a Universe, and all your hearts' desires. Dedicate yourself to your best and highest, and begin. What is the person you most desire to be–(I mean, freely, and honestly, not morally)? Imitate that person, and what began as imitation will end as perfection.

It is possible to cultivate habits of mind and of attention. The splendor of nature is all about us, immortal in loveliness, inexhaustible in wonder. The sky calls to us in the high places, the wind and the rain greet us, trees and grasses speak to us, mountains and the great plains and green valleys; we have only to open our minds and hearts to the eternal forces, and we and the eternal forces are one.

From such harmonies, the creative will draws force to inform the mind. He who has opened the way to nature will not wait long to know his own Way.

In the beginning, any consistent action dedicated to the discovery of the Will or to its development, suffices. The nature of an act is in no wise important, so long as it serves as a lever to set the Will in motion, and so long as it is repeatedly performed.

Almost any device is permissible if it helps. The use of a Talisman, fetish, or image symbolizing the Will; the use of a daily formula or ritual, and most especially the dedication of a certain period of every day, rain or shine, in sickness or health, in enthusiasm or loathing, for the exclusive practice of the dedicatory act. There is a danger; mind or muscle building as an end in itself can degenerate into a subtle form of masturbation.

The Will must be freed of its fetters. The ruthless examination and destruction of taboos, complexes, frustrations, dislikes, fears, and disgusts hostile to the will is essential to progress. Even in the case of pet preferences and prejudices, it must be realized that those things are only significant to the individual–meaningless and often silly to the larger world. On a hot day, Galahad probably stank under his armor. And that sensibility which is nauseated by the sex odor of its own kind, and titillated by the sex odor of plants, might be profitably studied under the heading of a perversion.

Now suppose that the second step is reached. The Will is beginning to flow. You know who you are, what you are, you have discovered your destiny.

It is time for rejoicing, but no for relaxation. There is no reason in nature why you cannot write music beyond Beethoven, poetry beyond Shelley, out-invent Edison, or out-theorize Einstein!

They are beacons, lighting the sky which you, in your own time and in your own way, will one day illumine.

The task is just begun. There is work ahead, years of work,–but work in the real world. Woe to him who dallies with escapist day dreams, with fancies and visions and trances, with specious words and poses, and the onanistic flatter of his fellow opium eaters.

The Will is creative and dynamic, and it must create and move in hard fact. By their fruits shall ye know them. Success is your proof;–but YOUR success, on your own terms. The way is hard; you will face failure after failure, fall after fall. But each fall and each failure is a success; a new jewel for the diadem of conscious experience.

Life–beautiful, terrible, splendid and pitiless;–Life is your adversary and your love. She you must accept unreservedly, and she you must overcome. She woos to destroy, she submits to conquer; she conquers to submit–that Tigress is your paramour, the Cosmos is your adventure.

And the goal? The totality of experience–the gesture commensurate with the universe.

Is that not enough?

Jack Parsons, a founder of the Jet Propulsion Laboratory in Pasadena, California, was a rocket scientist, occultist and member of Crowley's magical order. He died in 1952 in a mysterious laboratory explosion. His eloquent writings on the human condition convey passion, intelligence and a deep conviction.

OSHO (Bhagwan Shree) Rajneesh
Enlightened Master, Teacher and One of the
Greatest Religious Leaders of All Time

REBELLION IS THE BIGGEST "YES" YET

OSHO (Bhagwan Shree Rajneesh)

Author of the New Falcon Publication title:
Rebellion, Revolution & Religiousness

Beloved Master. All the historical rebellions have a huge "no" at their source. Your rebellion of the soul is centered in the mystery of "yes." *Will you please speak to us on the alchemy of "yes"?*

There are a few very fundamental things to be understood.

First, there has never been a rebellion in the past, only revolutions. And the distinction between a revolution and a rebellion is so vast that unless you understand the difference you will not be able to figure the way out of the puzzle of your question. Once you understand the difference...

Revolution is a crowd, a mob phenomenon. Revolution is a struggle for power: one class of people who are in power are thrown out by the other class of people who have been oppressed, exploited to such a point that now even death does not matter. They don't have anything. Revolution is a struggle between the haves and have-nots.

I am reminded of the last statement in the Communist Manifesto by Karl Marx. It is tremendously beautiful, and with a little change I can use it for my own purposes.

First its exact statement: he says, "Proletariate"–his word for the have-nots–Proletariat of the world unite, and don't be afraid because you have nothing to lose except your chains."

Moments come in history when a small group of people–cunning, clever–start exploiting the whole society. All the money goes on gathering on one side and all the poverty and starvation on the other. Naturally this state cannot be continued forever. Sooner or later those who have nothing are going to overthrow those who have all.

Revolution is a class action, it is a class struggle. It is basically political; it has nothing to do with religion, nothing to do with spirituality. And it is also violent, because those who have power are not going to lose their vested interest easily; it is going to be a bloody, violent struggle in which thousands, sometimes millions of people will die.

Just in the Russian Revolution thirty million people were killed. The czar's whole family–he was the king of Russia before the revolution–was killed by the revolutionaries so brutally that it is inconceivable. Even a six-month-old girl was also killed. Now, she was absolutely innocent, she had done no harm to anybody; but just because she belonged to the royal family... The whole royal family had to be destroyed completely. Seventeen people were killed, and not just killed but cut into pieces.

It is bound to happen in a revolution. Centuries of anger ultimately turn into blind violence.

And the last thing to remember: revolution changes nothing. It is a wheel: one class comes into power, others become powerless. But sooner or later the powerless are going to become the majority, because the powerful don't want to share their power, they want to have it in as few hands as possible.

Now, you cannot conceive in this country... There are nine hundred million people, but half the capital of the country is just in Bombay. Nine hundred million people in the whole country, and half the capital of the whole country is just in a small city. How long can it be tolerated? Revolution comes naturally, automatically–it is sometimes blind and mechanical, part of evolution. And when the powerful become the smaller group, the majority throws them away and another power group starts doing the same.

That's why I say revolution has never changed anything, or in other words, all the revolutions of history have failed. They promised much, but nothing came out of it. Even after seventy years, in the Soviet Union people are still not getting enough nourishment. Yes, there are no more the old czars and counts and countesses and princesses and princes–but in a vast ocean of poverty, even if you remove those who have power and riches it is not going to make the society rich; it is just like trying to make the ocean sweet by dropping teaspoonfuls of sugar in it.

All that has happened is a very strange phenomenon that nobody takes notice of. Only, poverty has been distributed equally: now in the Soviet Union everybody is equally poor. But what kind of revolution is this? The hope was that everybody would be equally rich.

But just by hoping you cannot become rich. Richness needs a totally different ideology of which mankind is absolutely unaware. For centuries it has praised poverty and condemned richness, comfort, luxury. Even it the poor revolt and come into power, they don't have any idea what to do with this power, how to generate energy to create more richness, comfort and luxury for the people. Because deep down in their minds there is a guilty feeling about richness, about luxury, about comfort.

So they are in a tremendous anguish, although they have come to power. This is the moment they could change the whole structure of the society, its whole productive idea. They could bring more technology; they could drop stupid kinds of wastage.

Every country is wasting almost ten percent of its income on the army. Even the poorest country, even this country is doing the same idiotic thing. Fifty percent of the people in this country are on the verge of any day becoming an Ethiopia, a bigger Ethiopia. In Ethiopia one thousand people were dying per day. The day India starts becoming another Ethiopia–and it is not far away–then one thousand will not do; it will be many thousands of people dying every day.

By the end of this century the population of India will be the biggest in the whole world. So far it has never been; it has always been China that was ahead. By the end of the century–and there are not many years left, just within twelve years we will be reaching the end–India will have one billion people. Five hundred million people are bound to die, because there is no food for so many people.

But still the politicians, those who are in power, are not concerned at all what happens to humanity. Their concern is whether power remains in their hands or not. The can sacrifice half of the country, but they will go on making efforts to have atomic weapons, nuclear missiles.

It is a very insane kind of society that we have created

in thousands of years. Its insanity has come now to a high peak. There is no going back. It seems we are all sitting on a volcano which can explode any moment.

Revolutions in the past have happened all around the world, but no revolution has succeeded in doing what it promised. It promised equality, without understanding the psychology of human individuality. Each human individual is so unique that to force them to equality is not going to make people happy, but utterly miserable.

I also love the idea of equality, but in a totally different way. My idea of equality is equal opportunity for all to be unique and themselves. Certainly they will be different from each other, and a society which does not have variety and differences is a very poor society. Variety brings beauty, richness, color.

But it has not yet dawned on the millions around the world that revolution has not helped, and they still go on thinking in terms of revolution. The have not understood anything from the history of man.

It is said that history repeats itself. I say it is not history that repeats itself; it only seems to repeat itself because man is absolutely unconscious and he goes on doing the same thing again and again without learning anything, without becoming mature, alert and aware.

When all the revolutions have failed some new door should be opened. There is no point in again and again changing the powerful into the powerless and the powerless into the powerful; this is a circle that goes on moving.

I don't preach revolution.

I am utterly against revolution.

I say unto you that my word for the future, and for those who are intelligent enough in the present, is *rebellion*.

What is the difference?

Rebellion is individual action; it has nothing to do with the crowd. Rebellion has nothing to do with politics, power, violence. Rebellion has something to do with changing your consciousness, your silence, your being. It is a spiritual metamorphosis.

And each individual passing through a rebellion is not fighting with anybody else, but is fighting only with his own darkness. Swords are not needed, bombs are not needed; what is needed is more alertness, more meditativeness, more love, more prayerfulness, more gratitude. Surrounded by all these qualities you are born anew.

I teach this new man, and this rebellion can become the womb for the new man I teach. We have tried collective efforts and they have failed. Now let us try individual efforts. And if one man becomes aflame with consciousness, joy and blissfulness, he will become contagious to many more.

Rebellion is a very silent phenomenon that will go on spreading without making any noise and without even leaving any footprints behind. It will move from heart to heart in deep silences, and the day it has reached to millions of people without any bloodshed, just the understanding of those millions of people will change our old primitive animalistic ways.

It will change our greed, and the day greed is gone there is no question of accumulating money. No revolution has been able to destroy greed; those who come into power become greedy.

We have passed through a revolution just now in this country, and it is a very significant example to understand. The people who were leading the revolution in this country against the British rule were followers of Mahatma Gandhi, who preached poverty, who preached non-possessiveness. The moment they came into power all his disciples started living in palaces which were made for viceroys. All his disciples who had been thinking their whole lives that they are servants of the people became masters of the people.

There is more corruption in this country than anywhere else. This is very strange–this is Gandhian corruption, very religious, very pious, and the people who are doing it were trained, disciplined to be servants of the people. But power has a tremendous capacity to change people; the moment you have power you are immediately a different person. You start behaving exactly like any other powerful person who have gone before.

Nothing has changed. Only the British are gone, and in their place a single party has been ruling for forty years. Now it is not just a single party, but a single family; it has become a dynasty. And the exploitation continues and the poverty continues–it has grown at least a hundred times more since the British Empire has been gone.

Everything has deteriorated–the morality, the character, the integrity, everything has become a commodity. You can purchase anybody; all you need is money. There is not a single individual in the whole country who is not a commodity in the marketplace; all you need is money. Everybody is purchasable–judges are purchasable, police commissioners are purchasable, politicians are purchasable. Even under the British rule this country has never known such corruption.

What has the country gained? The rulers have changed, but what does this signify? Unless there is a rebelliousness spreading from individual to individual, unless we can create an atmosphere of enlightenment around the world where greed will fall down on its own accord, where anger will not be possible, where violence will become impossible, where love will be just the way you live...where life should be respected, where the boy should be loved, appreciated, where comfort should not be condemned. It is natural to ask for comfort.

Even the trees... In Africa, trees grow very high; the same trees in India don't grow that high. I was puzzled, what happens? I was trying to find out why they should grow to the same height but they don't, and the reason I found was that unless there is a density of trees, trees won't grow high. Even at a lesser height the sun is available, and that is their comfort, that is their life, that is their joy. In Africa the jungles are so thick that every tree tries in every way to grow as high as possible, because only then can it have the joy of the sun, the joy of the rain, the joy of the wind. Only then can it dance; otherwise the is nothing but death.

The whole of nature wants comfort, the whole of nature wants all the luxury that is possible. But our religions have been teaching us against luxury, against comfort, against riches.

A man of enlightenment sees with clarity that is it unnatural to demand from people, "You should be content with your poverty, you should be content with your sicknesses, you should be content with all kinds of exploitation, you should be content and you should not try to rise higher, to reach to the sun and the rain and the wind." This is absolutely unnatural conditioning that we are all carrying. Only a rebellion in your being can bring you to this clarity.

You say that in history all the rebellions were based on "no." Those were not rebellions; change the word. All the revolutions were based on "no." They were negative, they were against something, they were destructive, they were revengeful and violent.

Certainly, my rebellion is based on "yes"–yes to existence, yes to nature, yes to yourself. Whatever the religions may be saying and whatever the ancient traditions may be saying, they are all saying no to yourself, no to nature, no to existence; they are all life-negative.

My rebellion is life-affirmative. I want you to dance and sing and love and live as intensely as possible and as totally as possible. In this total affirmation of life, in this absolute "yes" to nature we can bring a totally new earth and a totally new humanity into being.

The past was "no."

The future has to be "yes."

We have lived enough with the "no," we have suffered enough and there has been nothing but misery. I want people to be as joyful as birds singing in the morning, as colorful as flowers, as free as the bird on the wing with no bondages, with no conditioning, with no past–just an open future, an open sky and you can fly to the stars.

Because I am saying yes to life, all the no-sayers are against me, all over the world. My yes-saying goes against all the religions and against all the ideologies that have been forced upon man. My "yes" is my rebellion. The day you will also be able to say "yes" it will be your rebellion.

We can have rebellious people functioning together, but each will be an independent individual, not belonging to a political party or to a religious organization. Just out of freedom and out of love and out of the same beautiful "yes" we will meet. Our meeting will not be a contract, our meeting will not be in any way a surrender; our meeting will make every individual more individual. Supported by everybody else, our meeting will not take away freedom, will not enslave you; our meeting will give you more freedom, more support so that you can be stronger in your freedom. Long has been the slavery, and long has been our burden. We have become weak because of the thousands of years of darkness that have been poured on us.

The people who love to say "yes" who understand the meaning of rebellion, will not be alone; they will be individuals. But the people who are on the same path, fellow-travelers, friends, will be supporting each other in their meditativeness,, in their joy, in their dance, in their music. They will become a spiritual orchestra, where so many people are playing instruments but creating one music. So many people can be together and yet they may be creating the same consciousness, the same light, the same joy, the same fragrance.

It is a long way–"no" seems to be a shortcut–that's why it has not been tried up to now. Whenever I have discussed it with people, they said, "Perhaps you are right, but when will it be possible that the whole earth will say 'yes'?"

I said, "Anyway we have been on this earth for millions of years and you have been saying 'no'–and what is your achievement? It is time. Give a chace to 'yes' too."

My feeling is that "no" is a quality of death; "yes" is the very center of life. "No" had to fail because death cannot succeed, cannot be victorious over life. If we give a chance to "yes" based in rebelliousness it is bound to become a wildfire, because everybody deep down wants it to happen. I have not found a single person in my life who does not want to live a natural, relaxed peaceful, silent life.

But that life is possible only if everybody else is also living the same kind of life.

I can understand the fear of people that individual rebellion may take a long time, but there is no problem in it.

In fact each individual who passes through this rebellious fire becomes at least for himself a bliss and an ecstasy, and there is every possibility that he will sow the seeds around him. But he has not failed; he has conquered, he has reached to the very peak of his potential. He has blossomed. There is nothing more that he can think of; the whole existence is his.

So as far as that individual is concerned the rebellion is complete. He will be able to sow seeds all around. And there is no hurry; eternity is available. Slowly, slowly more and more people will become more and more conscious, more alert. Enlightenment will become a common phenomenon.

It should not be that only in a while there is a Gautam Buddha, once in a while there is a Jesus, once in a while there is a Socrates–the names can be counted on only ten fingers. This is simply unbelievable. It is as if our garden is full of rosebushes, thousands of rosebushes, and once in a while one rosebush blossoms and gives you roses. And the remaining thousands remain without flowers?

Unless a rosebush comes to blossom it cannot dance—for what? It cannot share; it has nothing to share. It remains poor, empty, meaningless. Whether it lived or not makes no difference.

The only difference is that when it blossoms and offers its songs and its flowers and its fragrance to existence and to anybody who is willing to receive, the rosebush is fulfilled. Its life has not been just a meaningless drag; it has become a beautiful dance full of songs, a deep fulfillment that goes to the very roots.

I am not worried about time. If the concept is understood, time is available; enough time is available.

In the East we have a beautiful proverb: The man who loses the path in the morning, if he returns home by evening he should not be called lost. What does it matter? In the morning he went astray—just little adventures here and there—and by the evening he is back home. A few people may have come a little earlier; he has come a little late, but he is not necessarily poorer than those who have come earlier. It may be just vice versa: he may be more experienced because he has gone wandering so far astray. And then coming back again, falling and getting up—he is not necessarily a loser.

So time is not at all a consideration to me.

My rebellion is absolutely individual and it will spread from individual to individual. Sometime this whole planet is bound to become enlightened. Idiots may try to wait and see what happens to others, but they also finally have to join the caravan.

The very idea of enlightenment is so new, although it is not something that has not been known before. There have been enlightened people, but they never brought enlightenment as a rebellion. That is what is new about it. They became enlightened, they became contented, they became fulfilled, and a great fallacy happened and I have to point it out. Although I feel not to show any mistakes of the enlightened ones–I feel sad about it–but my responsibility is not for the dead. My responsibility is for those who are alive and for those who will be coming.

So I have to make it clear. Gautam Buddha, Mahavira, Adinatha, Lao Tzu, Kabir, all those people who became enlightened attained to tremendous beauty, to great joy, to utter ecstasy–to what I have been calling *satyam, shivam, sundram*, the truth, the godliness of the truth and the beauty of that godliness.

But because they had become enlightened they started teaching people to be contented: "Remain peaceful, remain silent." This is the fallacy. They attained contentment after a long search. It was a conclusion, not a beginning; it was the very end product of their enlightenment, but they started telling people that you can be contented right now: "Be fulfilled, be silent."

That's how they became anti-rebellious, without perhaps knowing that if a poor man remains contented with his poverty it is dangerous; if a slave remains contented with his slavery, it is dangerous.

So all the enlightened people of the past attained to great heights, about which there is no doubt. But there is a fallacy that they all perpetuated without exception. The fallacy is that they began telling people to start with that which comes in the end. The flower comes only in the end; one has to start with the roots, with the seed. And if you tell people to start with the roses, then the only way is to purchase roses of plastic. The only way to be contented without meditation is to be a hypocrite, because deep down you are angry, deep down you are furious, deep down you want to freak out, and on the surface you are showing immense peace. This peace has been like a cancer to humanity.

You can see it happening in this country more clearly than anywhere else, because this country was fortunate, blessed by more enlightened people than any other country– but unfortunately, because so many enlightened people committed the same fallacy, this country remained for twenty centuries continuously a slave. This country has remained for centuries

"Hallelujah! came the response from the back.

The vicar managed to get to the end of the sermon, but at the end went up to the American and said, "Excuse me, I'm afraid in this country we like to keep a bit of decorum. We try to keep a stiff upper lip. It is the queen's own country, this is a place of God, and I frankly found your behavior rather disconcerting."

"Hey, man, I'm sorry, you are right on. I just loved the quaint way you gave us all that great shit about Moses and the Ten Commandments and I thought I would throw a few thousand greenbacks in your direction for this great thing going on here."

"Cool, man!" said the preacher.

It does not take much to find out what is deep inside. All decorum, all culture is so superficial; it will be a tremendous joy to see people in their authenticity, in their reality, without any decorum, without any make-up, just as they are. The world will be tremendously benefited if all this falseness disappears.

The alchemy of "yes" and the rebellion based on "yes" are capable of destroying all that is false, and discovering all that is real and has been covered for centuries, layer upon layer by every generation, so much that even you yourself have forgotten who you are.

If suddenly somebody wakes you up in the middle of the night and asks you, "Who are you?" you will take a little time to remember who you used to be the night before when you went to bed.

It happened that George Bernard Shaw was going to deliver a lecture some distance away from London. On the way in the train came the ticket-checker. George Bernard Shaw looked in every pocket, opened all his suitcases, but the ticket was not there. Finally, he was perspiring and the ticket-checker said, "Don't be worried, I know who you are; the whole country knows, the whole world knows. The ticket must be somewhere, you don't be worried. And even if its lost, I am here to help you get out of the station, wherever you want to get out."

George Bernard Shaw said, "Shut up! I am already in confusion and you are making me more confused. I am trying to remember where I am going! That ticket was the only thing...I am not searching for the ticket for you, idiot; I don't care about you, you can get lost. Bring me my ticket!"

The man said, "But how can I find your ticket?"

George Bernard Shaw said, "Then what am I supposed to do? Where should I get down? Because unless I know the name of the station..."

It is almost the same situation with everybody. You don't know who you are; your name is just a label that has been put upon you, it is not your being. Where are you going?– you don't have any ticket to show you where you are going to get down, and you are just hoping that somebody may push you somewhere, or maybe somewhere the terminus comes and the train stops and it does not go anywhere else... Just hoping.

But why are you traveling in the first place? In fact, for all those fundamental questions you have only one answer: I don't know. In this state of unawareness your revolutions cannot succeed. In this state of unawareness, your desire for freedom is just a dream. You cannot understand what freedom is. For whom are you asking freedom?

My idea of a rebellion based on "yes' means a rebellion based on meditation, for the first time in the history of man. And because each individual has to work upon himself, there is no question of any fight, there is no question of any organization, there is no question of any conspiracy, there is no question of planting bombs and hijacking airplanes.

I am not interested in hijacking airplanes, neither am I interested in destroying any governments. But it will be the final result of my individual rebellion based on meditation: government will disappear. They have to disappear; they have been nothing by a nuisance on the earth. Nations have to disappear. There is no need of any nations; the whole earth belongs to the whole of humanity. There is no need of any passports, there is no need of any visas.

This earth is ours, and what kind of freedom is there if we cannot even move? Everywhere there are barriers, every nation is a big imprisonment. Just because you cannot see the boundaries you think you are free. Just try to pass through the boundary and immediately you will be faced with a loaded gun: "Go back inside the prison. You belong in prison. You cannot enter into another prison without permission." These are your nations!

Certainly, a rebellion of my vision will take away all this garbage of nations, and discrimination between white and black, and give the whole of humanity a natural, relaxed, comfortable life. This is possible, because science has given us everything that we need, even if the population of the earth is three times more than it is today.

Just a little intelligence is needed–which will be released by meditation–and we can have a beautiful earth with beautiful people, and a multidimensional freedom which is not just a word in the dead constitution books but a living reality.

One thing finally to be remembered: the days of revolution are past. We have tried them many times, and every time the same story is repeated. Enough. Now something new is urgently needed. And except for the idea that I am giving you of a rebellion, individual and based on meditativeness, there is no other alternative proposed anywhere in the world.

And I am not a philosopher; I am absolutely pragmatic and practical. I am not only talking about meditative rebellion, I am preparing people for it. Whether you know it or not doesn't matter. Whoever comes close to me is going to become a rebellious individual, and wherever he will go he will spread this contagious health. It will make people aware of their dignity, it will make people aware of their potentiality. It will make people alert to what they can become, what they are, and why they are stuck.

My sannyasins' function is not to be missionaries, but to be so loving, compassionate, such fragrant individuals... It is not a question of converting people from one ideology to another ideology. It is a far deeper transformation–from the whole past to a totally new and unknown future. It is the greatest adventure that one can think of.

Satyam-Shivam-Sundram, Session 26, Nov. 19, 1987

Osho, known as Bhagwan Shree Rajneesh, was born in India in 1932 and died in 1990. He stands as one of the most famous, and to some, infamous, religious leaders of modern times. He probably hold the record for being thrown out of, or refused entry into, the greatest number of countries in history. His life and his work should be inspiration to rebels everywhere. For information contact Osho Commune International, 17 Koregaon Park, Poona 411 011, India.

Part II
The World of Chaos, Taboo and Transformation

Aleister Crowley

TABOO AND TRANSFORMATION IN THE WORK OF ALEISTER CROWLEY
Richard Kacynski, Ph.D.

Spiritual polymorph, sexual omnivore, psychedelic pioneer, and unapologetic social misfit, Aleister Crowely cut a scandalous figure in his Edwardian heyday. He was rediscovered during the counter-cultural revolution of the 1960s and beatified as a pop culture icon, with the groundswell of interest resulting from his renaissance yet to crest. While his detractors are as numerous as his admirers, to dismiss him as a mere hedonist is to ignore the ghost in the machine: As Gerald Yorke, Crowely's friend and *advocatus diabolus*, explained: "Crowley didn't *enjoy* his perversion! He performed them to overcome his horror of them."[1] Yorke's is no disingenuous revisionist memoir. Throughout Crowley's corpus runs of the idea of spiritual transformation by plunging into one's phobias and philias.

The ceremonial magick championed by Crowley and his forebears in the Golden Dawn is, in a nutshell, alchemy: The transformation of one's base character into spiritual gold. Crowley sought to improve upon this High Art by channeling

---

[1] Fuller, Jeanne Overton. The Magical Dilemma of Victor Neuburg. London: W.H. Allen, 1965, p. 244.

human nature's most powerful drives into a form of sexual alchemy. His rationale, while not using this language, boils down to a simple thesis: If psychological triggers can precipitate spiritual change, then the taboos socially programmed into us can act as triggers for major spiritual transformation. Thus, Crowley spent his life probing the impulses against which guilt, sin or plain common sense dissuaded most.

This behavior found its earliest expression in what Crowley admits is a defining moment of his childhood:

> I must have been about 6 years old. I was capering around my father during a walk through the meadows. He pointed out a branch of nettles in the corner of the field, close to the gate (I can see it quite clearly today!) and told me that if I touched them they would sting. Some word, gesture, or expression of mine caused him to add: Would you rather be told, or learn by experience? I replied, instantly, I would rather learn by experience. Suiting the action to the word, I dashed forward, plunged in the clump, and learnt.
>
> This incident is the key to the puzzle of my character.[1]

From there, the exploration of ill-advised impulses became a constant quest. Thanks to his fundamentalist upbringing in the Plymouth Brethren faith, an abundance of taboos presented themselves. Simply reading the wrong book was a potential misstep for the young Crowley. By his teenage years, he had discovered the "Three Evil Kings," i.e., Drin-King, Smo-King and Wan-King.

---

[1] Crowley, Aleister. Chapter LVII. Beings I Have Seen with My Physical Eye. *Magick Without Tears*. New Jersey: Thelema Publishing Co., 1954; rpt. Tempe, AZ: New Falcon Publications.

By the time Crowley entered Trinity College, he understood the hazards of gratuitous sensuality. His second book, the notorious *White Stains* (1898), emulated the Decadent art and literature of his social circle. Critics, then as well as today, twittered at such suggestive titles as "A Ballad of Passive Paederasty" and "With Dog and Dame," oblivious to the cautionary tale underlying the risqué subject matter: The book's protagonist finds the thrill of his mild erotic quirks waning over time, driving him to more extreme vices which ultimately culminates in madness and murder. At its core, the book is a critique of hedonism.

Despite the moral of *White Stains*, Crowley wrestled with his own young adult drives. Long periods of abstinence–proscribed for magicians by medieval grimoires–proved counterproductive. While abstaining, sexual urges didn't dissipate, they consumed him. Rather than slowly starve the impulse to death, Crowley concluded a better strategy was simply to appease it and get on with the Great Work. He considered sex an impulse like thirst or hunger, best divorced from the emotional baggage which society attached to it. Later he would remark, "The stupidity of having had to waste uncounted priceless hours in chasing what ought to have been brought to the back door every evening with the milk![1] Alas, these countless priceless hours gained him a reputation whose repercussions he would suffer repeatedly throughout his lifetime: In 1900, on the basis of his character, he was barred from further advancement in the Hermetic Order of the Golden Dawn. Thus purposive indulgence collided with prudishness, and its eidolon was Queen Victoria.

---

[1] Crowley, Aleister. *Confessions of Aleister Crowley.* London: Hill & Wang, 1969, p. 113.

Despite a childhood aversion to England's monarch, he admitted that "I was brought up in the faith that Queen Victoria would never die."[2] She symbolized the spirit of the age, where respectability and propriety was imposed on all expressions, both public and private. Social stagnation, Crowely believed, was rooted in this hypocritical and risible hyper-morality. It was in this context that Crowley and his climbing colleague, Oscar Eckenstien, "broke into shouts of joy and an impromptu war dance"[3] upon learning of Queen Victoria's death in 1901. By the time he wrote *The World's Tragedy* in February of 1909, his disdain had crystallized:

> Priests who are celibates–outside of choir!
> Maidens who rave in Lesbian desire:
> The buck of sixty, cunning as a trapper,
> Stalking the pig-tailed, masturbating flapper;
> The creeping Jesus–Caution! we must shock it!_
> With one hand through his turn-out breeches pocket;
> Flagellants shrieking in our streets and schools,
> Our men all hogs, and all our women ghouls:–
> This is our England, pious dame and prude,
> Who calls me blasphemous, unchaste, and rude![4]

By the end of 1909, Crowley began to realize the magical potential of sex. He was in Africa with his student Victor Neuburg, conducting a series of visionary experiments which would become The Vision and the Voice. While attempting to skry into the 14th of the 30 Enochian Aethyrs,

---

[2] Chapter LXXVII. Work Worth While: Why? *Magick Without Tears*, See also an indentical remark in *Confessions*, p. 41.
[3] *Confessions*, p. 216.
[4] Crowley, Aleister. *The World's Tragedy.* Paris: privately printed, 1910, p. XXXVII; 2nd ed. Phoenix: New Falcon Publications, 1992.

Crowley found his progress blocked. Seized with inspiration, the magicians built a makeshift altar to the Greek god Pan and consecrated it with a sex act. Although Crowley was promiscuous, Neuburg was only his second male lover. The first, from his college days, left him with feelings of sin and guilt. This time, the homosexual encounter–in the open air under the desert sun, to the service of the Great Work–profoundly impacted him. He felt his ego–the Aleister Crowley raised in Victorian England by Plymouth Brethren parents–dissolve. In the language of initiation, he had crossed the Abyss.

Thus his attitude toward sex progressed significantly in the decade between entering college and writing *The Vision and the Voice*. In his original view, the reproductive impulse was a distraction from spiritual work, and was best sated to maximize the amount of time the mind could devote to higher goals. By 1909, he realized that the socially constructed boundaries called morality could literally block spiritual growth. By breaching taboos, Crowley realized he could break down these barriers, countermanding his social programming. This is what a later generation of rebels and devils would call "undoing yourself."[1]

Crowley's 1912 meeting with Theodor Reuss, head of the Ordo Templi Orientis, forged the last link in this chain of thought. In this legendary encounter, Reuss accused Crowley of revealing the O.T.O's central secret in *The Book of Lies*. When Crowley claimed innocence, Reuss directed him

---

[1] Hyatt, Christopher S. *Undoing Yourself with Energized Meditation and Other Devices*. 6th printing. Tempe, AZ; New Falcon Publications, 1993.
——, *Undoing Yourself Too*. Tempe, AZ; New Falcon Publications, 1998.

to Chapter 36, "The Star Sapphire." Reading the words, "Let the Adept be armed with his Magick Rood [and provided with his Mystic Rose.]" with the understanding that Reuss interpreted these words as sexual symbols, the light bulb lit. The chain was completed. Sex was not merely a distraction from the Great Work, nor merely a barrier to advancement. It was the very vehicle of a potent form of magick which replaced the traditional claptrap with our own bodies.

To be fair, Crowley was already heading in this direction, as documented in the Abuldiz working, The *Scented Garden*, and *Liber Stellae Rubeae*.[1] But the Reuss encounter gathered those thoughts into coherent form. From this point, Crowley vigorously engaged not only in ritual sex[2] but other taboo experiences, all in the pursuit of spiritual insight.

Thus, when he took up painting around 1917, he advertised for "Dwarfs, Hunchbacks, Tattooed Women, Harrison Fisher Girls, Freaks of All Sorts, Coloured Women only if exceptionally ugly or deformed, to pose for artist." When he founded his Abbey of Thelema in Cefalù, Italy, in 1920, he took a page from Paul Gaugin and made the walls his canvas. The result was *La Chambre des Cauchemas* (Chamber of Nightmares), whose murals bombarded viewers with an

---

[1] Crowley, Aleister. Liber LX: The Ab-ul-Diz Working. *The Vision and the Voice with Commentary and Other Papers*. York Beach: Weiser, 1998, p. 287-337.

——· *The Scented Garden of Abdullah the Satirist of Shiraz*, (Bagh-i-muattar). London, 1910:rpt Chicago: Teitan Press, 1991.

——·Liber Stellae Rubeae sub figura LXVI. *The Equinox I*, (7). 1912, p. 29-36.

[2] Symonds, John, and Grant, Kenneth. (eds). *The Magical Record of the Beast 666*. Quebec: Next Step, 1972; rpt. London: Duckworth, 1983.

array of frightful, disturbing and sexually explicit images. Crowley told visitors:

> There, in the corner, are Lesbians as large as life. Why do you feel shocked and turn away: or perhaps overtly turn to look again? Because, though you may have thought of such things, you have been afraid to face them. Drag all such thoughts into the light... 'Tis only your mind that feels any wrong... Freud endeavors to break down such complexes in order to put the subconscious mind into a bourgeois respectability. That is wrong–the complexes should be broken down to give the sub-conscious will a chance to express itself freely..."[1]

Karl Germer, visiting the Abbey in 1926, confirmed the cathartic intent of these murals. "Beast evidently did all that as a medicine...against the English disease *par excellance*."[2]

Having fleshed out his psychological theory of magick, he began explaining it to his students. As Frank Bennett recounts his visit to Cefalù,

> [H]e began to talk about initiation, and said it was a matter of getting the sub-conscious mind at work, that when this subconscious mind was allowed to have full sway, without interference with the physical mind, illumination began for he said this subconscious mind was our Holy Guardian. He illustrated this by saying that everything was felt in this mind, and it is constantly urging its will upon the physical mind, and when these impressions, or inner desires, are restricted or suppressed, evil and all kind of trouble are the result.[3]

---

[1] Captain J.H.E. Townsend to J.F.C. Fuller, 19 April 1921, Harry Ransom Humanities Research Center, University of Texas at Austin.
[2] Karl Germer to Norman Mudd, 4 February 1926, Binder New 116, Yorke Collection, Warburg Institute, University of London.
[3] Frank Bennett. (1921). Magical Record of Frater Progradior in a Retirement at. Cefalu Sicily. Yorke Collection.

While Crowley disagreed with psychoanalysis,[1] this etiological theory or "evil and all kind of trouble" paraphrases Freud's ideas regarding repression, sublimation and neurosis.

He also experimented with drugs at this time, making them accessible to the Abbey's visitors to rob them of their mystique and allure. His view on drug addiction paralleled *White Stains*' warning about sex, and, by extension, apply to all behaviors driven by the pleasure principle: Anything pursued hedonistically ultimately leads to moral collapse; but placing it in service to the Will protects the magician from addiction or other apostasies.[2] This calls to mind *The Book of the Law's* instruction, "To worship me take wine and strange drugs whereof I will tell my prophet, & he be drunk thereof! They shall not harm ye at all." (*AL* ii.22). On this passage, Crowley cautioned:

> Lest there be folly, let me say that this passage does not license reckless debauch. The use of drugs and drink is to be strictly and act of Magick. Compare what is said in the First Chapter with regard to the use of the functions of sex.[3]

---

[1] Crowley, Aleister. An improvement upon psychoanalysis. *Vanity Fair*, December 1916, p. 60, 137; rpt. Hymenaeus Beta and Richard Kaczynski (eds.)., *The Revival of Magick and Other Essays*. Tempe, AZ: New Falcon, 1998.

[2] Crowley, Aleister. *The Diary of a Drug Fiend*. London: W. Collins & Co., 1922.

―――· The great drug delusion. A New York Specialist (pseud.) *The English Review*, July 1922, p. 65-70.

―――·The drug panic. A London Physician (pseud). *The English Review*, (7). 1912, p. 29-36.

―――· Crowley found these principles harder than expected to put into practice in *Liber Tzaba vel Nike (The Fountain of Hyacinth)*, Binder A4-A5, Yorke Collection.

[3] Crowley, Aleister. Duplicate typescript with mss corrections of part of the unpublished commentary on the 'Book of the Law,' Oasis of Nefta, Al-Djerid, Tunisia, 1923. Rare Books Department, Z. Smith Reynolds Library, Wake Forest University, Winston-Salem, N.C.

Thus he reiterated that explorations of the human psyche's dark underbelly be intentional and purposive.

Other experiments at Cefalù involved gender bending, the *menage a trois*, sado-masochism and coprophagia. While Crowley considered this legitimate psychological research, he realized the controversial nature of his work. Between the publication of *The Diary of a Drug Fiend* and the unfortunate death from typhoid of an Abbey visitor, the tabloids of the time unleased an astonishing series of attacks. Crowley's reaction:

> I regard all these people, all England with rare individual exceptions, as moral cowards with all that that implies. Sir Richard Burton had an experience precisely similar to mine. So had Christopher Columbus. So had Darwin. Their instinctive dread of a man who dares the unknown. *Omne Ignotum pro terribili* and such a man may bring it to their door at any moment. The whole history of science illustrates this. Science is now tolerated because Science has been at pains to prove that (on the balance) it has benefited mankind. I, bringing as I do, new knowledge of the unknown, and obviously the mark of fear, horror and persecution.[1]

Small wonder that Crowley's records from Cefalù were seized and destroyed by H.M. Customs as pornographic when he tried returning them to England.

In the end, Crowley became the eidolon or reflection of those impulses denied by society which Queen Victoria symbolized. Confronting the Beast meant confronting those repressed impulses, with the resulting ordeal dubbed "The Vision of the Demon Crowley." Indeed, those who persevered and

---

[1] Aleister Crowley to Norman Mudd, 20 April 1924, Yorke Collection.

saw through the smoke screen became his staunchest advocates–Gerald Yorke, Louis Wilkinson, Karl Germer and Israel Regardie among them–while those who bolted off were convinced they had narrowly escaped the clutches of the devil. "The main danger seems to be getting caught on the reef of his own interpretation," Kenneth Grant commented. "But this, after all, is but the proper function of the 'Demon Crowley'!"[1] Likewise, when Crowley began a campaign to rehabilitate his reputation, Gerald Yorke neatly summarized the function of the Great Beast:

> To my mind, part of your 'mission,' if I may use a word I mistrust, is to show that the code of morals of what a Thelemite calls the Old Aeon has been superseded, and that now any act is right provided it is done in the right way, as in interpretation of True Will. It must have been your Will to be the Beast, and a whitewashed Beast is an useless commercial article.[2]

Crowley must have been convinced, for he continued living the rest of his life with no apologies.

Analogues in Other Traditions

The notion of sacrifice–literally to make sacred, or to find the holy in the mundane–is not unique to Crowley.

Hasidic Jews find God through the "enjoyable and necessary acts of ordinary life."[3] Early forms of Hasidism's *Chabad* mysticism included practices like *Haalat ha-Nitzotzot* ("elevating the sparks," or recognizing everything

---

[1] Kenneth Grant, private communication, 5 December 1989.
[2] Gerald Yorke to Aleister Crowley, 20 March 1928, Binder New 116, Yorke Collection.
[3] Cantor, Norman F. *The Sacred Chain: The History of the Jews.* New York: Schocken, 1988.

as a manifestation of God), *'Avodah he-Hipukh* ("worship through inversion," where self-fulfillment comes from joining things–even God–with its opposite), and its extension *Yeridah Le-Tsorekh 'Aliyah* ("descent for the purpose of ascent"). When the *Tzaddikim* began discussing things like the sanctity of sin, exploring the *Sitra Ahra* (the "opposite tree" or *Qlippoth*), or discussing how one can find God by exploring the desire to kill one's neighbor, these practices were eliminated as dangerous.[1]

In Tantra, followers of the *Kaula* branch and *vama marg* or "left hand path" advocate the well-known *panchamakaras* or *panchatattva* ritual. Literally meaning "five elements," it involves partaking five substances which are usually religiously prohibited. The five items, in Sanskrit, all begin with the letter M; hence, this ritual is often referred to as "the five M's." The items are *madya* or *madir*–(wine or liquor), *matsya* (fish), *m–msa* (meat), *mudr*–(parched grain) and *maithun*–(sex, often out of caste). The concept behind this ritual is that which drove Crowley's explorations: Social taboos, broken in a religious context, can produce great spiritual advancement.[2]

---

[1] Ariel, David S. *The Mystic Quest: An Introduction to Jewish Mysticism.* New York: Schocken, 1988..

Elior, Rachel. *The Paradoxical Ascent to God: The Kabbalistic Theosophy of Habad Hasidism.* New York: State University of New York Press, 1993.

[2] Garrison, Omar. *Tantra: The Yoga of Sex.* New York: Causeway, 1964.

Feuerstein, Georg. *Tantra: The Path of Ecstasy.* Boston: Shambhala, 1998.

Douglas, Nik, and Slinger, Penny. Sexual Secrets: *The Alchemy of Ecstasy.* New York: Destiny, 1979; rpt. New York: Inner Traditions, 1989.

Finally the masters known as the Aghori represent such an extreme manifestation of this formula that they are the object of fear and awe in India, believed to have transcended all boundaries of good and evil. Their best-known activities center around mankind's greatest taboo, death. *Aghori* will sleep in cemeteries, often sharing the same coffin with corpses. They observe and wait, ready to celebrate the popping of the body's skullcap, for to them that represents the final release of the soul. Once or twice in a lifetime, an *Aghori* will consume a piece of human brain, the first place to show the stirrings of the spirit and the last place from which it is vacated. Even necrophilia is not unknown.[1] By immersing themselves in the most dreaded of all things–human death and decay–the *Aghorii* seek not only to come to terms with death, but also–like Crowley, the *Chabad* mystics and the *Tantrikas*–to come a little closer to understanding God.

---

[1] Svoboda, Robert E. *Aghora: At the Left Hand of God*. Brotherhood of Life: Albuquerque, NM, 1986.

Richard Kaczynski, Ph.D. is a psychologist specializing in non-mainsteam religious beliefs. He has written extensively and lectured internationally on mystical and magical beliefs and practices.

UNDOING YOURSELF WITH CHAOS MAGICK
Robert F. Williams, Jr.

What follows is geared toward those new to Chaos Magic and for those struggling along in so-called magical organizations that study magic but can't seem to actually do anything magical. It is also for those who are pouring over old magical texts searching for the secrets of magic, trying to unearth a ritual that really works, and instead find themselves uncovering information that is not understandable or pertinent and is basically just plain useless.

A good starting point if you have been discourage by this type of time wasting and are ready for a change, is to read the work of present day alternative thinkers like William S. Burroughs, Timothy Leary, Robert Anton Wilson, Philip K. Dick, Christopher S. Hyatt, Phil Hine and Israel Regardie. If you are already reading some of this stuff, that is even better–don't stop! Once you've begun you'll find that one god author seems to guide you to the next. They will help you to begin looking at things from a divergent point of view. Mutating your perspective is an excellent beginning for the transformation necessary to become a Chaos Magician. A new way of viewing things is an important starting point and yet it is only the starting point–Chaos Magic demands action.

Chaos Magic can be distinguished from other forms of magic by several basic tenets. These I will get into in just a moment. I would first like to make clear one differentiation as it relates to this subject. Many concepts in Chaos Magic are "simple"; however, when I say "simple" I do not mean "easy'. Chaos Magic is about change, both in the restructuring of the mind and in the world in which we live. Once you've begun to work with Chaos Magic you will discover it really does work, that is to say, you will realize that you are actually capable of manipulating your outer existence as well as your internal reality. When you reach this point the big question will become: "Now that I can change, what am I going to change to?" This issue is more than just a philosophical exploration; it becomes an actuality that has to be faced.

Self-directed change implies achievement, and yet the simple words "change" has ramifications that are staggering to most people. In fact most people are allergic to change–by that I mean the average person will, without any real inner reflection, place themselves in a routine and stay in that routine as long as possible. Sometimes these routines are not pleasant. We see these people everywhere, trapped in lives of alcoholism, drug addiction, bad marriages, job problems or whatever. People stay in these routines rather than face making a change. People tend to continue these behaviors as long as possible and they will, at all costs, avoid honestly looking at themselves and avoid any opportunity to try something different. This brings to mind a quote from one of my heroes, Ralph Waldo Emerson, who once noted "foolish consistency is the hobgloblin of little minds." Even the smallest life changes, such as being forced to take a minor detour from the normal route to work, can ruin an entire morning for most little minded people. Are you one?

For the Chaos Magician change, even for the sake of change, is better than no change at all. For lack of change leads to stagnation and to stagnate is to die. Changes such as assuming different viewpoints, being open to different belief systems and to at least temporarily accept new ideas, doing things differently, all of these imply movement from one belief to another belief point. This movement can produce momentum, and momentum, guided by purpose–unencumbered by doctrine and presuppositions–can produce the desire of the directed will. This, then, indicates a successful magical act. A magical act may be defined as causing reality to conform to the will.

"Belief is a technique" is one of the basic tenants of Chaos Magic and we can use any belief system that appeals to us. The point is that this new-found belief has to be established as (a temporary) reality and it has to be believed in as fully as possible while it is being used. Basically we pretend that something is true until it works. Belief can be used to trick the Subconscious or Unconscious into accepting that something is real, then the Subconscious, which has almost unlimited power, goes about bringing this condition into reality. While we are using a belief it is important to do everything possible to trick the Unconscious and convince it that your belief is a reality. One of the ways this can be done is to act the part, dress the part, talk and live the part of the belief that is being used. Basically "act as if" until the belief becomes a reality. It is far easier to act your way into changed thinking than it is to think your way into changed action. If you dress someone up as a soldier, make them march around like a soldier, have them carry a rifle and bark martial orders at them, they will soon believe that they are a soldier and thus become a soldier. Military leaders have known this for centuries.

A symbolized representation of the desire is more functional and will burn more clearly and be less obstructed in the Subconscious than a consciously thought out desire will work or can be maintained in the Conscious mind. The Unconscious mind understands and performs in response to symbolic representations of desire. Carl Jung was aware of this and so was a magician named Austin Osman Spare. Although Spare referred to Jung and Freud as "Junk and Fraud," his magical system was influenced by both men's ideas. Spare realized and understood the power of the Unconscious. He also understood the potential of the Conscious to interfere with realizing its potential. He therefore created a system that allowed him to sneak information past the Conscious and plant it into the Unconscious.

The Unconscious mind responds best to symbols of desire. Using symbols that have been created by another or that are very old or are written in some foreign language are not any more effective than those that you create yourself–in fact the opposite may be true. Your effort to create your own symbol or "alphabet of desire" means that both your Conscious and Unconscious mind are fully aware of what you have been up to. This fact in itself allows you a personal relationship with your work. I would rather sleep in my own bed, or drive my own car than someone else's. This holds true for your personal symbols and the feeling of familiarity. Self-created symbols allow you to resonate with something that is a part of you and therefore is more effective.

Creating your own symbolized desire is no harder than knowing what your desire is (and that is the hardest part), writing it out as "IT IS MY WILL TO...!" Once this has been done, you may use any method you wish to convert this desire into a symbol. Combine the letters, make a drawn or written representation, juxtapose the words into a mantram that disguises its original meaning, shape into a clay talisman or whatever—your method is only limited by your own imagination.

An altered state of consciousness (gnosis) is an essential factor for this magical procedure to achieve its successful consummation. The Conscious must be distracted from the desire so the desire can move into the Unconscious and be properly seeded. The Conscious mind actually will interfere with the work if it is allowed to participate. The Conscious mind cannot be counted on to hold a clear image of desire, let alone to actually send the desire out into the aether to cause change. If you have ever tried to hold a singular image or thought in your mind and not allow any other thoughts or images to enter, you understand how difficult this is. The conscious mind cannot stand being limited to such and it will do all in its power to fight this process. If you have any doubt try thinking of your front door knob and nothing else for three minutes. Good luck.

The Subconscious is the most powerful and change-effecting. If a sharp, clear image of your desire is planted into your Subconscious it will burn there indefinitely sending information to the world within and outside of you to effect the desired change. Not only is the Unconscious powerful, it is a reservoir of all information that is taken in. It contains the entire store of all information that has been assimilated through the course of our lives. Within the Subconscious resides snatches of all the foreign languages we've heard, all the mathematical equations we've been taught, and all the sights, sounds, smells, and feelings of everything that we have experienced from the first day we went to kindergarten, the moment of our birth, before birth, to now. The sum total of everything that we have ever perceived both consciously and unconsciously is stored here. This information is very useful when doing Divination.

The point is that the Conscious mind must be fully occupied or distracted while planting the seed (casting the spell) into your Unconscious. The most effective way of achieving this is to alter your conscious state. The two opposite ends of the spectrum of altered consciousness are to fire the mind up into an extreme state of excitement or bring it to a state of total calmness. These have been represented by magicians as a volcano and a pool of calm water, Fire and Ice, Death and Sex, Thantos and Eros. This is how the magical society The Illuminates of Thanateros arrived at its name, illumination though the ritual use of sex and death states of consciousness. These states may be achieved by various methods.

The ritual need not be complicated although elaborate ritual work, can be fun and is definitely beneficial in terms of distracting the Conscious mind away from the true desire–in other words it will help you overcome, as Crowley put it, "the lust of result."

First you decide your desire and create a symbol to represent it. Then you banis and go about achieving an altered state: you can dance, drum, have sex, spin in circles, hyperventilate, stare into a mirror, focus on a single spot on the wall, meditate or hypnotize yourself. Your path to the top of the mountain is your own. After some experimenting you will find what is most effective for you. When you have reached the peak of altered consciousness, or mind distraction, it is time to recall and *strongly visualize* the symbolized representation of your desire. Do *not* think about the desire itself–in fact, forget the desire–and see only the symbolized representation. Visualize this in your mind's eye as long as possible and then let it go and forget the desire. It is important not to let the Conscious mind interfere with what you have just done. When you have finished, banish once again.

Quantum Theory may help explain how this process works. A Conscious belief as a symbolized desire actually manifests as information in the Subconscious. Quantum Theory would indicate that information has a shaping effect on matter and the world around us. With Chaos Mathematics and Chaos Theory it is thought that the Universe is chaotic and random as opposed to ordered and governed by strict laws. At any given moment any number of possible futures could manifest and in fact might exist simultaneously. Information from this moment couples with one of the possible futures that it has an affinity for and shapes it into a probability, thus encouraging it to be more likely to happen. If you make something more likely to happen you are literally forcing the hand of chance or causing reality to conform to will...Magic!

Robert F. Williams, Jr. was one of the founding members of the Illuminates of Thanateros in the United States. He was a contributing author to several books and magazines. His tragic death, shortly before the first edition of this book sent to press, shocked and saddened us all.

Photo by Harry Widoff / Bookateria.com

DEVIL BE MY GOD

Lon Milo DuQuette

Author (or co-author) of the New Falcon Publication titles:
The Enochian World of Aleister Crowley: Enochian Sex Magic
Sex Magick, Tantra and Tarot: The Way of the Secret Lover
Aleister Crowley's Illustrated Goetia: Sexual Evocation

"I advise you to curb that waging tongue of yours."
–Bishop of the Black Connons

"It's a habit I've never formed Your Grace."
–Robin Hood

In A.D. 415 Cyril, the Bishop of Alexandria Egypt, found himself in a most awkward position. Not only was he burdened with the task of concocting viable doctrines[1] from the muddled and conflicting traditions of the young Christian cult, he was required to do so in the most sophisticated and enlightened pagan city on earth.

Long before the alleged virgin birth of the crucified savior, Alexandria, with her celebrated schools and library, nurtured the greatest minds of the Mediterranean world and Asia. Here, religion and philosophy were lovers, and their union gave rise

---

[1] Cyril is credited with formulating the concept of the Holy Trinity, an invention for which he was eventually canonized.

to dynamic environment of dialog and debate. On more than one occasion Cyril tried to glean converts from the student body of the Neo-Platonic Academy, only to be stuck dumb by the discomforting realization that the fledgling philosophers were far more knowledgeable than he about the subtleties and shortcomings of his own faith. Uncomfortable as he such moments were His Grace bore them dutifully. They afforded him the opportunity to suffer for his faith. His patience came to an end, however, when his faith and reputation were challenged by a brilliant and charismatic luminary of the Alexandrian School of Neo-Platonism, Hypatia–the greatest woman initiate of the ancient world.

Hypatia of Alexandria was without question the most respected and influential thinker of her day. The daughter of the great mathematician, Theon, she took over her father's honored position at the Academy and lectured there for many years. She, more than any other individual since Plotinus, the father of Neo-Platonism, grasped the profound potential of that school of thought. Her lectures were wildly popular and attracted a stream of scholars who was in Ne-Platonism the possibility of a truly universal spiritual order–a supreme philosophy–an enlightened religion to unite all religions. Such was the golden promise of Neo-Platonism, and Hypatia of Alexandria was its virgin prophetess.

Troubled by the continued degeneration of the Christian movement, its intolerance of other faiths and its dangerous preoccupation with miracles and wonders, Hypatia began a series of public lectures dealing with the cult. She revealed the pagan roots of the faith and systematically unmasked the absurdities and superstitions that had infected the movement. Then, with power and eloquence surpassing that of any Christian apologist, she elucidated upon what she understood to be the true spiritual treasures found in the purported teachings of the "Christ."

Her arguments were so persuasive that many new converts to the cult renounced their conversions and became disciples of Hapatia. Her lectures stimulated enormous interest in Christianity, but not Christianity as it was presented by Cyril, the Bishop of Alexandria.

Not blessed with the strength of character necessary to suffer a personal confrontation with Hypatia, Cryil embarked upon a campaign of personal vilification by preaching to his unwashed and fanatical flock that Hypatia was a menace to the faith, a sorceress in league with the Devil. These diatribes seemed to have little effect upon the sophisticated population of urban Alexandria who were beginning to realize that Bishop Cyril's Christianity was a cult that didn't play well with other children. Deep in the Nitrian dessert, however, Cyril's hateful words eventually reached the crude monastery of Peter the Reader.

Years of preaching to the wind and converting scorpions had uniquely qualified Peter to be the cleansing sword of the Prince of Peace, and the though of a devil-possessed woman attacking his savior was more than this man of God could stomach. Mustering a rag-tag collection of fellow hermits, he marched to Alexandria where they met with officials of the Caesarean church who informed him that each afternoon the shameless Hypatia drove her own chariot from the Academy to her home. Armed only with clubs, oyster shells, and the Grace of God, Peter and his mob ambushed Hypatia in the street near the Academy. Pulling her from her chariot they dragged her to the Caesarean church where they stripped her, beat her with clubs, and finally (because of an on-going debate over the soul's eternal status if the corpse remained whole) scraped the flesh from her bones with the oyster shells. The scoops of flesh and the rest of her remains were then carried away and burned.

The reaction of the Alexandrian community was one of confusion and shock, and the Neo-Platonist school was dealt a blow from which it never recovered. Although he went to great lengths to distance himself from the incident, Cyril took full advantage of the situation and used the terror of the moment to further intimidate the city and establish that the will of the Christian God was to be resisted at one's own risk.

The martyrdom of Hypatia was certainly not the first example of truth resisting evil and losing, but it did mark the beginning of a prolonged spiritual delirium tremor from which Western Civilization has never fully recovered. Even the bright souls who did not succumb to the universal madness were forced to blossom against the twisted projections of the collective nightmare.

Spiritual growth is not impossible in such an environment. But where wisdom is perceived by the world to be ignorance; love is considered sin, and all that is best in the human spirit is condemned and repressed, the road by which a seeker of enlightenment must travel takes many curious turns. On such a journey one's companions are outlaws and rebels; sacredness breeds in blaspheme, truth falls from the lips of false prophets, heaven is sought in hell, and God is the Devil himself.

Lon Milo DuQuette is a noted Tantric authority who has written and taught extensively in the areas of Mysticism, Magick and Tarot.

THE BLACK ART OF PSYCHOTHERAPY
Dr. Jack S. Willis

The multi entendre of the title is intentional and appropriate (multi: more than double, less than many). Let us count the ways.

First, psychotherapy is an art. It is not a science (the human-beings-are-laboratory-rats mentality of the behaviorists notwithstanding). A friend of mine, a philosopher of esthetics, defines art as: anything that people treat as art. So it is with psychotherapy. Any mad school that springs up and that gets people to call it "psychotherapy" then becomes a "psychotherapy." But is it good psychotherapy or just mad? We will return to that.

Second of the entendre is that, by whatever definition, it is a black art. And, in two ways. First, it supposedly deals with the dark side of the person. Call it dark, call it hidden, call it black; by whatever name, it is the devil within us that is awakened in psychotherapy. Second, as an art, it is dependent not only on the artistry of the practitioner, but also no the (en)light (enment) of the therapist. We will return to that, too.

Third of the entendre, it is a black art because, examined closely, it employs the same techniques, albeit in different robes, as does thaumaturgy and invocation of the spirits. The names of the spirits are different, and the drugs are (usually) different, and the invocation rituals are different; but it is magic nonetheless. And black magic at that.

Do you wish to move to a different plane of consciousness? Try hypnosis or alpha wave biofeedback or sodium amytal or any number of emotion altering drugs. Do you wish to feel fully? Try Gestalt or psycho-drama or Primal. Do you wish to probe the unknown and unknowable. Try Jungian. Do you wish a re-birth? Try Rankian, or rebirthing, or age regression (even to rebirth in former lives). Do you wish to be loved? Try Rogerian. Is death your issue? Existentialist therapy awaits. Or, perhaps you want better sex or mind-body unity? Try Reichian, Bio-energetics, Feldenkrais, Rolf or Alexander technique. For every passion there is a therapy, and for every therapy there is a passonate following. What to do? What to do? We will return to that, too. There is an answer.

Final of the entendre, it is also an art of the patient (really a student rather than a patient). The art of the student is where we will finish our exploration.

Psychotherapy As Art

No two people are alike. A photograph as art can be duplicated an infinite number of times. Similarly an etching. A bronze can be recast. But people are ever unique and ever changing. The interchange between therapist and student is a ballet. Is there a leader and a follower? The can be; there doesn't have to be. But one thing of this dance is certain: if the therapist can only dance to his own tune, if he is committed to a school and a technique irrespective of the student, then the ballet will be an awkward and even disasterous performance.

How then does the student choose a teacher? How can you judge your teachers artistic sensibility? I will answer the choice of teacher question here and wait until later to address the question of his artistry. The answer to choosing a teacher is easy, if not obvious. There are two questions to ask: (1) what is your objective and (2) what is your time line. Put it this way: if you exercise, do you want a little workout once or twice a week or do you want to really tone your muscles? Do you want to exercise until you lose 10 pounds, or do you want to make it a part of your life? What is your objective and what is your time line? If your objective is limited and/or you want quick answers, then choose a teacher whose method is quick and direct. Rational emotive therapy, hypnosis, cognitive-behavioral or behaviorism are good answers.

If your objective is to increase your happiness quotient, to correct your errors in living, to exercise the daemons inside you, then choose a teacher who increases anxiety. If your teacher promises to love you unconditionally, run. If your teacher tells you that he is problem oriented, run. If your teacher tells you that he will deal with your emotions but not with your thinking, run. If he says he deals with the here-and-now not with the past, sprint. If he says he is only a (fill in the school) therapist and that is the only school he believes in, find a new teacher. There is no sense in finding a teacher of French when you are planning a trip to Germany.

But, since nothing in life is easy, if he says he is totally flexible, that he is eclectic, that he uses whatever is appropriate with no commitment to any theory, then make a mad dash. In psychotherapy, the word eclectic is often a synonym "for I don't know what I am doing, I just do whatever feels right."

If your objective is long-term personal growth, then choose the teacher whose statement to you make you anxious, unsettled, nervous, unsure. Therein lies an answer.

The Dark Side of Our Soul

I will make the, I think very reasonable, assumption that anyone who reads this book is interested in maximizing their potential and increasing their productivity and creativity. For such a person therapy is a Godsend (to steal a metaphor). My teacher, Israel Regardie (and Dr. Hyatt) said that he would not teach anyone the methods of the Golden Dawn unless they had had at least 4 years of Reichian therapy. Regardie took that position for a very good reason. Until we have removed some of the darkness within our own soul, any attempt at thaumaturgy will only evoke our own indwelling devils. Freud said that repression and sublimation were necessary for one to live in the society. Reich claimed the only answer was to change society. I am less pessimistic then those two towering figures.

When they were writing, we did not have the knowledge of the developmental steps of the ego and we did not have the work of Piaget on children's cognitive development. I've proven it enough times to enough students; that I can say with some confidence that the main issue in our personal psychology is mistakes in thinking. As children we attempted to understand the silly (sometimes crazy, sometimes evil) statement and actions of our parents. However, children and adults live in different worlds of knowledge and thinking. What seems obvious to a parent, is adult babble to a child. Parents pretend that they are teaching the child to …(behave, to considerate, share, be polite, etc.) when in truth all they are doing is confusing the child. The child tries to make sense out of the teaching, misunderstands most of what is taught; and neither the child nor the parent knows how off the two are.[1]

Human beings are magnificent but flawed creatures. We take the mistakes of childhood, we live them our whole life, we never recognize they were wrong to begin with, and that they are now doubly wrong as adults. Thus we live our lives in war with ourselves. It is a terrible waste of energy. We take the glory and the beauty of the infant and create anger and misery of the adult. It is to take a David of Michelangelo and re-sculpt him into a Henry Moore burdened and struggling tortured soul.

It doesn't need to be, it shouldn't be. Freud said, where the id was, there the ego shall be. I would say where darkness was there light shall be.

The (En)Light(enment) Of The Therapist

There is a danger in psychotherapy. The danger is called the therapist. The therapist is the magician of this black art. When he attempts to exorcise your devils is he doing it by inserting his own? In psychological terms, is he attempting to project his own devils into you? And how can you tell if he is?

There is no infallible answer to this one. There are some guides. How much therapy has your proposed therapist had (minimum of 7 years)? What kind of therapy(ies) did he have? Is he attempting to use a particular school of therapy in which he has not himself been a patient If so, choose another teacher.

---

[1] My favorite story is the mother who yells at her child to not play with the lamp because he will break it. A moment later, and CRASH! So, "I told you not to play with the lamp, now look what you've done!" But, says the bright child, "I wasn't playing with the lamp, I was playing with the spaceship." Children live in different cognitive universes than do adults.

You can ignore licenses and degrees. They mean nothing. What matters is the knowledge of and therapy experience of your proposed therapist, not what degrees or licenses he does or does not have. In how many schools of therapy is he knowledgeable? The minimum is two. But here is the most important rule of all: if the therapist talks about himself (other than to answer your questions) or he frequently brings in how he feels or would feel in your situation then he is definitely trying to work out his own problems on your time. You have come upon a dark soul (irrespective of or in spite of any therapy he may have had). Stop now. You are with the wrong teacher. Darkness can not create lightness of being.

Choosing A Therapist

It may seem like I have talked of little else. But the subject is not exhausted. As a Reichian therapist of nearly 30 years experience, there is more that can be added. As you may know, Reichian therapy is a body approach to therapy. Therefore, we get a lot of information from the physical appearance, the gestures, the voice tone, the eyes, etc. Here, then, are some tips from the Reichian couch. Your therapist should have forehead creases. The should not be permanent (a furrowed brow), they should become prominent when the eyebrows are raised and, except or the crease, disappear when the eyebrows are lowered. His eyes should be clear, very focused, and they should move easily. There should be a definite nasal-labial line (the line from the corner of the nose to the corner of the mouth). The neck muscles should not be prominent. The voice should be resonant, coming firm an open throat rather than a constricted one. If he takes a big breath, both the belly and the chest should move. Of the things I have listed here, the most important is the forehead and the eyes. If his eyes are dull or they do not move easily or his forehead has no crease lines or has permanent creases, quit now. What if you have been making wonderful progress with just this kind of therapist? My suggestion: take a six-month vacation from this therapist and look into some others. The vacation will be good for you anyway and the experience of some visits to other teachers might give you some perspective on his virtues and his failings.

If you have not chosen a therapist, or if you are going to take a vacation, here is my suggestion: There are four good schools of depth therapy: psychodynamic, ego psychology (also called object relations), neo-Freudian, and Reichian. Note that the word is *psychodynamic*, not *psychoanalysis*. The foundation is the same, but the technique is very different. Notwithstanding that Jungian is very popular among the readers of New Falcon Publications, I would urge against it. I have yet to see good results emerge from Jungian analysis. Stay as far away as possible from Primal therapy or any variant. Adlerian, in the right hands, is an acceptable alternative; but then go to someone else afterwards to get to the areas that Adlerian can not address. Bio-energetics is not bad except that you walk around angry for years, in the process losing marriages, jobs, and friends. Existential therapy can be done well, but it is rare. Most therapists proclaiming themselves as existentialist have not done the study necessary to make good use of the art. Existentialist is not one school; it is a whole bunch with differing degrees of worth. Of all the rest, I would say: Ignore them. They are not depth therapy, and they can not do the job you deserve.

The Art Of The Patient

Now, finally, to the most important part: **YOU!** Even a truly good teacher is no good if the student will not study, if the student will not do his homework. If you are not important to your self why should you be important to your therapist? Is it rational to expect that your therapist will work hard for you when you will not work hard for yourself?

Here is a statement that you have probably never heard any therapist make: the two most important qualities that you need to bring to the study are anger and courage. Anger in the form of the demand of yourself, the commitment, that you will not settle for less than you can be. You will not settle for injuring your children because you have not uncovered your own daemons. You will not settle for less productivity, less creativity, less enjoyment of the wonder of life than is possible for you to achieve. That does not mean that your goal is perfection. We leave that realm to the Gods. It does mean that however much you can uncover, understand, and correct is the minimum you will settle for and the devil take the hindmost.

Then there is courage. Daemons are scary creatures. What are your daemons? Are they depression, anxiety, anger, guilt, facing the fact that your parents are not the nice people you want them to be, realizing that you have been living your life for other people and not for yourself, realizing that you are not as important as you want to think you are, realizing that you made a bad choice in a mate, realizing that you have been pretending to enjoy sex? For all your determination to surrender the darkness for the light, you have to have the courage to stay the course, confess the big and the little, accept that you are what you are–not what you want to be, and most of all: the determination to accept that the losses of your childhood are permanent losses. That last one is a biggie and it raises another factor.

Intellectual integrity should be another part of your art. A man of intellectual integrity does not attempt to fake reality.

What is, is. It is not subject to our fantasies, our wishes, or our ideals. It is not pretty or ugly. It is not noble or ignoble. It is not heroic or cowardly. It simply is. As honesty is telling the truth to others, so integrity is telling the truth to ourselves. It is much harder. We know when we are lying to someone else. But the lies we tell our self are the lies we live by. They are part of our very being. And they are corrosive.

There is much that could be said here, but there is only one thing I want to add. Never accept anything your therapist says except as a possibility to honestly examine. Your own mind is the ultimate judge of the validity of any idea or interpretation. Yes, you are student to this teacher because you can not uncover your own errors of thinking. But the alternative is not to turn your mind over to someone else.

Your therapist may or may not be an advanced soul, an enlightened person. He may have penetrating insights, and he may be "a wise man" (as the Talmudists would say). And, certainly, you are in his office to take a graduate degree in living. Certainly his explanations and interpretations deserve a respectful audience. But, in the end, it is our trained judgment that is the authority. Your therapist can demand all he wants that he is right because he is the therapist/authority. Do not buy it. On the subject of you, you are the authority. Take every idea he puts forth, examine it with anger, courage, and integrity, and then, if it is wrong, discard it. Your life is a temple. It deserves respect, reverence, and prayer; don't let it go to waste, it is too sacred.

Dr. Jack S. Willis has graduate degrees in Biochemistry and Psychology and a Doctor of Chiropractic. He trained in Reichian Therapy with Dr. Israel Regardie for nine years. He is director of the Reichian Therapy Center in Los Angeles, California. The Reichian Therapy Center is both a treating and teaching institute.

The Social Epidemic of child abuse

★★★

THE CURSING OF OUR CHILDREN

Chapter 1 from The Social Epidemic of Child Abuse

Dr. William S. Hyatt, Ph.D.
New Falcon Publications 2022

Verbal Abuse: Our Exposed, Secret Shame

The Effects of a Declining Culture on the Mental Health of Our Children

No child has ever signed a contract to be born.

How children are treated and regarded is the best metaphor that **reflects** the true moral development of a culture.

When asked what type of adults we want our children to become, we say one thing.

When we observe how our children are raised, we see a different paradigm being applied.

When we observe how our children turn out, we revert back to our original model of expectation.

We frequently explain away this glaring disparity by denying our failure and blaming the young adult, thus reinforcing the entire socialization process–itself schizophrenic in nature–and which a puritanical and at the same time hedonistic America is so famous for throughout the world.

We single out America because it claims to be loving and forgiving; it claims to be the best; setting the world standard of excellence in every facet of human life. From economics to socialization; from production methods to technology. (Forget "Science", the discovery of new knowledge and the creations that spring from it; the products of an enlightened people. We never had "Science" and never will. We have "technology": the bigger faster, cheaper, more of the same basis of excess consumption.) Americans also **believe** we should export goods; are also **determined** we should export our "values." And when our "values" are rejected by other cultures, we then extol the "might makes right" excuse to use force to insure our concept of "human rights" for all, while our own society spirals ever further down into the abyss of a cesspool.

But the fact is, as our daily newspaper headings show, America trains its citizens to be **violent, deceptive and abusive**. Not simply to ourselves and to adult peers, but to children. In reality "The American Dream" promises, violence, deception, and abuse is **the** way! Everyone "knows".. **how else can you be successful?**

No Child Can Say "No" To Abuse

When I was a young child and someone called me a name, I would say, "Sticks and Stones will break my bones, but names will never hurt me." But the fact is, names did hurt me. But the pain was hidden. It had to be hidden, and I was the one who **had** to do the hiding. After all, I was taught it was a sign of weakness to let others know their purposely designed cruel words "Hurt!" And if for some reason, I "lost my senses" and opened myself up to them and let them know of my pain, I risked the further pain of humiliation by the "cowardly act" of letting them know that I was hurt and wounded by what someone said. It was not until the mid 1960s that a daring realization began to enter the minds of a few perceptive, analytically-minded individuals: that **words have as much**

power to produce an effect on a human being as does a physical force on a material object. After all, words are very real forces arising within the brain. They can be displayed on the cathode ray screen of an oscilloscope, and charted to a strip-chart recorder's paper. In short, they are a form of **energy**. And as such, they have the power to elicit emotions: the physically-based, chemical **effect** of the thought that **caused** it. In turn, these emotions produce actions by effecting the neuro-physical basis of our nervous systems, which then drive the rest of our material bodies to act on physical reality. Knowing this, all controlling societies apply this knowledge to create fear in their citizens. They do this through the use of fantasy and imagination, not so thinly veiled in their propaganda based, guilt structured, dependency-oriented legal system, itself generated by the socially determined edicts of the "chosen few," whose names and faces neither we will never know or see. In so doing, they guarantee obedience by the cheapest of all possible methods; since words are free.

From a more workable daily point of view, words or "names" are the basis or soil from which many human interactions spring. Sociology, psycholinguistics, hypnosis, neuro-linguistics, semantics, and propaganda have realized the overwhelming power of language in determining human behavior. In fact, Psychologists use words as their primary method of understanding, analyzing, and treating the mental causes that lie behind behavioral disturbances...or the physical "acting out" of these "thought-energy" generated effects.

If You Do Not Believe in the Popularity of Psychological Abuse, Then Turn On Your Television

And yet with all this theoretical and applied knowledge, little is said about the effects of words on the outcome of our child rearing practices; except of course, to refrain from swearing, demonstrating the most flagrant sexual actions, and editing the most violent and brutal movies.

The reason for this? Because all of us are guilty...in one way or the other...of abusing others with our own words.

While words may be cheap and always at the ready, they are nonetheless more powerful than we care to realize or admit...**especially** to ourselves.

> *"Words are everything and everything is words."*
> –Sheriff Leroy Baca
> Four time elected Sheriff of Los Angeles County

Words As a Component of Psychological Abuse

Unlike the ever-prevailing stereotype that portrays minorities and the poor as the exclusive social elements behind physical and mental child abuse, it is our position that Psychological Abuse has no social status whatsoever and neither does it have any cultural boundaries. Rather, it is our contention that such abuse is actually the most common form of derision indulged in by the middle and upper classes. The tragedy of this of course, is that unlike physical scars that heal, the insidious effects of psychological abuse remain buried in the psyche, often festering for decades, disturbing all elements of the individual's life throughout his or her entire lifespan.

It is the power of psychological abuse to so invade the entire field of a child's life and mutate, thus producing a plethora of negative thought patterns, that simply pointing a finger at specific "incidents" as "common examples" has become a nearly impossible. Surprisingly, in most cases, victims of such abuse are not even aware that they have been abused. This miasmatic characteristic of the abuse–while certainly not the most graphic and horrifying form of injury–is yet the most permanent and devastating of all forms of pain; simply because it is both non-incidental and nebulous at the same time. And being amazingly common, it does not lend itself to either simple investigation or healing. In fact, psychological abuse is as normal in America as cannibalism is in some primitive, tropical societies. The operational focus behind this analogy then, is that ***the abusive-arrogant American does not regard his or her behavior as deviant, anymore than does the cannibal.***

Psychological Abuse is So Common in America That It Has Become a Way of Life

Psychological abuse has become a way of life in America. Its practice–and its consequences–are everywhere. As a long time coach, I have never been a guest in someone's home– where I did not observe psychological child abuse in one form or another. I well remember observing a mother calling her 3-month old child a "bad boy," simply because he was throwing up his milk. The woman was white, intelligent, and had a college degree, and financial means.

Having experienced life for so many decades, in anything but a "social vacuum," I have seen children beaten, humiliated, called derogatory names, belittled in front of other children and with adults present–simply because the parents were embarrassed by the child's behavior in what they considered to be a "public" setting. What does it communicate to us, about ourselves–as individual beings–and as a so-called "cultured, advanced civilization," when professionals and journalists agree that the "reprimand" (abuse) of a child is "required," and simply argue as to whether it is best to spank the child or simply scold it? What does it tell us about "loving" parents who demand respect because they do not have the courage to deal with their own shame, or handle their adult-centered problems in a mature, rational way? *These* are the "adults" the child is to look up to and later, emulate? Is our stature as human beings so insignificant, that emotional pigmies are giants compared to us?

Psychological abuse—whether in the home, on the job, or in the street—is so rampant and accepted as "normal," that we do not recognize it as an illness; as a disease that is destroying the very values and ideals which we mouth as being so important to our "civilized" way of life.

Animal Welfare Is More Important Than Child Welfare In Mainstream America

In this "America," there appears to be more public concern about animal welfare than the effects of psychological abuse. The slightest physical or even verbal reinforcement needed to train an animal so it can live among human beings without causing harm to them or their property, has seen legislation of one form or another enacted: all from "Animal Rights Activists" determined to "stop the abuse!" Yet these same "activists" think nothing of deriding, insulting, and down casting their own offspring in order to "train" them to live "properly" among the same set of human beings they are–in effect–protecting their animals from!

At times, clinicians, bureaucrats, and other so-called "socially responsible" and "politically correct" individuals and groups, refer to the progress made in child welfare by referring to Public Law 93–237 which defines abuse and neglect as:

> the physical or mental injury, sexual abuse, negligent treatment, or maltreatment of a child under the age of eighteen, by a person who is responsible for the child's welfare under circumstances which indicate that the child's health or welfare is harmed or threatened thereby.

It is true that this law acknowledges the issue; but in our opinion, this acknowledgment is both microscopically narrow and caustically vague. "Narrow," in that this law primarily implies parental or family abuse; "vague," in that the guidelines that detail the **content: that which actually constitutes** "abuse," is left as a matter of individual interpretation. In addition, these laws and many others dealing with this issue are woefully lacking, in that they do not adequately cover the abuse sanctioned by agencies, or society at large. Further... and most appalling of all—is that they do not emphasize ***psychological violence*** as the most common form of abuse. And finally, it is our contention here, that this and other so-called "Public Laws" do not provide for adequate remedies so drastically needed to turn the tide of this incredible social epidemic.

> *"Unconditional love is the vaccine*
> *against all future dysfunction."*
> Dr. William S. Hyatt, Ph.D.

Part III

Reprogramming The Self

Timothy Leary, Ph.D.
World famous Psychologist, Writer and Philosopher

TWENTY-TWO ALTERNATIVES TO INVOLUNTARY DEATH

Timothy Leary, Ph.D. & Eric Gullichsen

Author of the New Falcon Publication title:
What Does WoMan Want?
The Intelligence Agents
The Game of Life
Info-Psychology
Neuropolitique

"Death is the ultimate negative patient health outcome."
–William L. Roper, Director, Health Care Financing Administration (HCFA), which administers Medicare

Most human beings face death with an "attitude" of helplessness, either resigned or fearful. Neither of these submissive, often uninformed, "angles of approach" to the most crucial event of one's life can be ennobling.

Today, there are many practical options available for dealing with dying process. Passivity, failure to learn about them, might be the ultimate irretrievable blunder. Pascal's famous no-lose wager about the existence of God translates into modern life as a no-risk gamble on the prowess of technology.

For millennia the fear of death has depreciated individual confidence and increased dependence on authority.

True, the loyal member of a familial or racial gene-pool can take pride in the successes and survival tenacity of their kin-ship.

But for the individual, the traditional prospects are less than exalted. Let's be laser-honest here. How can you be proud of your past achievements, walk tall in the present or zap enthusiastically into the future if, awaiting you implacably around some future corner, is Old Mr. D., The Grim Reaper?

What a PR job the Word Makers did to build this Death Concept into a Prime-Time Horror Show! The grave. Mortification. Extinction. Breakdown. Catastrophe. Doom. Finish. Fatality. Malignancy. Necrology. Obituary. The end.

Note the calculated negativity. To die is to croak, to give up the ghost, to bite the dust, to kick the bucket, to perish. To become inanimate, lifeless, defunct, extinct, moribund, cadaverous, necrotic. A corpse, a stiff, a cadaver, a relic, food for worms, a *corpus delicti*, a carcass. What a miserable ending to the game of life!

Fear Of Death Was An Evolutionary Necessity In The Past

In the past, the reflexive genetic duty of TOP MANAGEMENT (those in social control of the various gene-pools) has been to make humans feel weak, helpless, and dependent in the face of death. The good of the race or nation was ensured at the cost of the sacrifice of the individual.

Obedience and submission was rewarded on a time-payment plan. For his/her devotion the individual was promised immortality in the post-mortem hive-center variously known as "heaven," "paradise," or the "Kingdom of the Lord." In order to maintain the attitude of dedication, the gene-pool managers had to control the "dying reflexes," orchestrate the trigger-stimuli that activate the "death circuits" of the brain. This was accomplished through rituals that imprint dependence and docility when the "dying alarm bells" go off in the brain.

Perhaps we can better understand this imprinting mechanism by considering another set of "rituals," those by which human hives manage the conception-reproduction reflexes. A discussion of these is less likely to alarm you. And the mechanisms of control imposed by the operation of social machinery are similar in the two cases. We invite you to "step outside the system" for a moment, to vividly see what is ordinarily invisible because it is so entrenched in our expectation.

At adolescence each kinship group provides rituals, taboos, ethical prescriptions to guide the all-important sperm-egg situation.

Management by the individual of the horny DNA machinery is always a threat to hive inbreeding. Dress, grooming, dating, courtship, contraception, and abortion patterns are fanatically conventionalized in tribal and feudal societies. Personal innovation is sternly condemned and ostracized. Industrial democracies vary in the sexual freedom allowed individuals. But in totalitarian states, China and Iran for example, rigid prudish morality controls the mating reflexes and governs boy-girl relations. Under the Chinese dictator Mao, "romance" was forbidden because it weakened dedication to the state, i.e., the local gene-pool. If teenagers pilot and select their own mating, then they will be more likely to fertilize outside the hive, more likely to insist on directing their own lives, and, worst of all, less likely to rear their offspring with blind gene-pool loyalty.

Even more rigid social-imprinting rituals guard the "dying reflexes." Hive control of "death" responses is taken for granted in all pre-cybernetic societies.

In the past this conservative degradation of individuality was an evolutionary virtue.

During epochs of species stability, when the tribal, feudal and industrial technologies were being mastered and fine-tuned, wisdom was centered in the gene-pool stored in the collective linguistic-consciousness, the racial data-base of the hive.

Since individual life was short, brutish, aimless, what a singular learned was nearly irrelevant. The world was changing so slowly that knowledge could only be embodied in the species. Lacking the technologies for the personal mastery of transmission and storage of information, the individual was simply too slow, too small, to matter. Loyalty to the racial collective was the virtue. Creativity, Premature Individuation, was anti-evolutionary. A weirdo, mutant distraction. Only Village Idiots would try to commit independent, unauthorized thought.

In the feudal and industrial eras, Management used the fear of death to motivate and control individuals. Today, politicians use the death-dealing military and the police and capital punishment to protect the social order. Organized religion maintains its power and wealth by orchestrating and exaggerating the fear of death.

Among the many things that the Pope, the Ayatollah, and Fundamentalist Protestants agree on: confident understanding and self-directed mastery of the dying process is the last thing to be allowed to the individual. The very notion of *Cybernetic Post-Biological Intelligence* or consumer immortality-options is taboo, sinful. For formerly valid reasons of gene-pool protection.

Religions have cleverly monopolized the rituals of dying to increase control over the superstitious. Throughout history the priests and mullahs have swarmed around the expiring human like black vultures. Death belonging to them.

As we grow in the 20th century we are systematically programmed about How to Die. Hospitals are staffed with priests/ministers/rabbis ready to perform the "last rites." Every army unit has its Catholic Chaplin to administer the Sacrament of Extreme Unction (what a phrase, really!) to the expiring solider. The Ayatollah, Chief Mullah of the Islamic Death Cult, sends his teenage soldiers into the Iraq minefields with dog-tags guaranteeing immediate transfer to the Allah's Destination Resort. Koranic Heaven. A terrible auto crash? Call the medics! Call the priest! Call the Reverend!

In the Industrial Society, everything becomes part of Big Business. Dying involves Blue Cross, Medicare, Health Care Delivery Systems, the Health Care Financing Administration (HCFA), terminal patient wards. Undertakers. Cemeteries. The funeral rituals.

The monopolies of religion and the assembly lines of Top Management process dying and the dead even more efficiently than the living.

We recall that knowledge and selective choice about such gene-pool issues as conception, test-tube fertilization, pregnancy, abortion is dangerous enough to the church-fathers.

But suicide, right-to-die concepts, euthanasia, out-of-body-experiences, occult experimentation, astral-travel scenarios, death/rebirth reports, extra-terrestrial speculation, cryogenics, sperm-banks, egg-banks, DNA banks, personally-empowering Artificial Intelligence Technology–anything that encourages the individual to engage in personal speculation and experimentation with immortality–is anathema to the orthodox Seed-Shepherds of the feudal and industrial ages.

Why? Because if the flock doesn't fear death, then the grip of Religious and Political Management is broken. The power of the gene-pool is threatened. And when control looses in the gene-pool, dangerous genetic innovations and mutational visions tend to emerge.

Some believe that the Cybernetic Age we are entering could mark the beginning of a period of enlightened and intelligent individualism, a time unique in history when technology is available to individuals to support a huge diversity of personalized lifestyles and cultures, a world of diverse, interacting social groups whose initial-founding membership is one.[1]

The exploding technology of computation and communication lays a delicious feast of knowledge and personal choice within our easy grasp. Under such conditions, the operating wisdom and control naturally passes from aeons-old power of gene pools, and locates in the rapidly self-modifying brains of individuals capable of dealing with an ever-accelerating rate of change.

---

[1] The authors divide the stages of human history into: tribal, feudal, industrial, and cybernetic. The arrival of the latter stage is heralded in the authors' book *Cybernetic Societies*, to appear.

Aided by customized, personally-programmed quantum-linguistic appliances, the individual can choose his/her own social genetic future. And perhaps choose not to "die."

The Wave Theory Of Evolution

Current theories of genetics suggest that evolution, like everything else in the universe, comes in waves.

So, at times of Punctuated Evolution, collective metamorphosis, when many things are mutating at the same time, then the ten commandments of the "old ones" become ten more suggestions...

At such times of rapid innovation and collective mutation, conservative hive dogma can be dangerous, suicidal. Individual experimentation and exploration, the thoughtful methodical scientific challenging of taboos, becomes the key to the survival of the gene-school.

Now, as we enter the Cybernetic Age, we arrive at a new wisdom which broadens our definition of personal immortality and gene-pool survival: *The Post-Biological Options Of The Information Species*. A fascinating set of gourmet-consumer choices suddenly appear on the pop-up menu of The Evolutionary Cafe.

It is beginning to look as though in the Information Society, the individual human being can script, produce, direct his/her own immortality.

Here we face Mutation Shock in its most panicky form. And, as we have done in understanding earlier mutations, the first step is to develop a new language. We should not impose our values or vocabulary of the past species upon the new Cybernetic Culture.

Would you let the buzz-words of a preliterate paleolithic cult control your life? Will you let the superstitions of a tribal-village culture (now represented by the Pope and the Ayatollah) shuffle you off the scene? Will you let the mechanical planned obsolescence tactics of the Factory Culture manage your existence?

So let us have no more pious wimp-sheep talk about death. The time has come to talk cheerfully and joke sassily about personal responsibility for managing the dying process. For starters let's de-mystify death and develop alternative metaphors for consciousness leaving the body. Let us speculate good-naturedly about post-biological options. Let's be bold about opening up a broad spectrum of Club-Med post-biological possibilities.

For starters, let's replace the word "death" with the more neutral, precise, scientific term: *Metabolic Coma*. And then let's go on to suggest that this temporary state of "coma" might be replaced by: Auto-Metamorphosis, a self-controlled change in bodily form, where the individual chooses to change his/her vehicle of existence without loss of consciousness.

Then, let's distinguish between involuntary and voluntary metabolic coma. Reversible and irreversible dying.

Let's explore that fascinating "no-man's land"–the period between body-death and neurological-death in terms of the knowledge-information processing involved.

And let's collect some data about that even more intriguing zone now beginning to be researched in the cross-disciplinary field of scientific study known as Artificial Life.[1]

---

[1] Los Alamos, famous s the birthplace of atomic weapons, today also houses the Center of Nonlinear Studies, where a group has been meeting weekly to discuss the many technical aspects of the newly identified field

What knowledge-information processing capabilities can be preserved after both metabolic coma and brain cessation? What natural and artificial systems, from the growth of mineral structures to the self-reproduction of formal mathematical automata, are promising alternative candidates to biology for the support of life?

And then let us perform the ultimate act of Human Intelligence. Let's venture with calm, open-minded tolerance and scientific rigor into that perennially mysterious *terra incognita* and ask the final question: What knowledge-information processing possibilities can remain after the cessation of all biological life: somatic, neurological and genetic?

How can human consciousness be supported in hardware outside of the moist envelop of graceful, attractive, pleasure-filled meat we now inhabit? How can the organic, carbon-constructed caterpillar become the silicon butterfly?

C.S. Hyatt, Ph.D. and A.K. O'Shea have suggested three stages of *Post-Biological Intelligence*:

1. *Cybernetic Recognition* of the myriad knowledge-information processing varieties involved in the many stages of dying.

2. *Cybernetic Management*, developing knowledge-information processing skills while out-of-body, out-of-brain, and beyond DNA.

3. *Cybernetic-Technological*, Attaining one, or many, of the immortality options.

---

of Artificial Life. The center recently sponsored a week-long international workshop, the world's first, where scientists met to discuss the implications and craft the foundational theories of the field.

The meeting was friendly, fun, and wildly trans-disciplinary. Nanotechnology pioneers outlined the potential for protein engineering, and robotics expert Hans Moravec presented compelling arguments that a genetic takeover was underway, our cultural artifacts now evolving past the point of symbiosis with the human species. Self-replicating structures ranging from minerals to computer viruses were demonstrated.

Post-Biological Recognition Intelligence

We recognize that the dying process, for millennia has been blanketed by taboo and primitive superstition, has suddenly become accessible to human intelligence.

Here we experience the sudden insights that we need not "go quietly" and passively into the dark night or the neon-lit, musak-enhanced Disney-heaven of the PTL crowd. We realize that the concept of involuntary, irreversible metabolic coma known as death is a feudal superstition, a marketing efficiency of industrial society. We understand that one can discover dozens of active, creative alternatives to going belly-up clutching the company logo of the Christian Cross, Blue Cross, Crescent Cross, or the eligibility card of the Veterans Administration.

Recognition is always the beginning of the possibility for change. Once we comprehend that "death" can be defined as a problem of knowledge-information processing capacities around as long as possible. In bodily form. In neural form. In the silicon circuitry and magnetic storage media of today's computers. In molecular form, through the atom-stacking of nanotechnology in tomorrow's computers. In cryogenic form. In the form of stored data, legend, myth. In the form of off-spring who are cybernetically trained to use *Post Biological Intelligence*. In the form of post-biological gene-pools, info-pools, advanced viral forms resident in world computer networks and cyberspace matrices of the sort described in the "sprawl novels" of William Gibson.[1]

---

[1] William Gidson, cyberpunk psy-fi visionary, has published *Neuromancer*, *Count Zero* and *Burning Chrome*. They are recommended reading for their technically and socially plausible vision of high-tech low-life on the streets.

The second step in attaining Post-Biological Recognition Intelligence is to shift from the passive to the active mode. Industrial age humans were trained to await docilely the onset of termination and then to turn over their body for disposal to the priests and the factory (hospital) technicians.

Our species is now developing the Cybernetic Information Skills to plan ahead, to make one's will prevail. The smart thing to do is to see dying as a change in the implementation of information-processing: to orchestrate it, manage it, anticipate and exercise the many available options.

BREAKING TRANCE
Steven Heller, Ph.D.

Author of the New Falcon Publication title:
*Monsters and Magical Sticks:
There's No Such Thing As Hypnosis?*

How do you know when you're getting too close to a fire? Of course, by feeling the heat! But what if you were unable to feel the heat? You would probably not know until you were burning yourself or you smelled your flesh burning. So many people go through life in such a deep trance, that they do not know when they are heading for trouble until they have stepped into it. They no longer know what they feel, want or need!

A small child hears his/her parents fighting and becomes afraid. They tell conflicting stories and she/he becomes confused. They send out incongruent messages and the anxiety rises to painful levels. One day she/he discovers that by "dropping out" and going off into inner-space-out, everything is better... for a while. If I can't feel it, hear it or see it, it can't get me. TRANCE IS BORN! Of course, if a truck is coming at you and you respond by "Not seeing or hearing it" I guarantee that you will feel it. Your trance will simply prevent you from getting out of the way.

A child enters a new and exciting world called school. S/he is curious and open to learning. "Children, we must all sit just like this and always raise your hand and there is one right way to do things and of course only one right answer!" says the adult called teacher. Day in and day out s/he sees things but is told they don't really exist. S/he feels things and is told that the feelings are not real and s/he doesn't really know what s/he feels in the first place. The secret of survival? Go into a trance! The result...years later s/he doesn't feel what there is to feel, can't hear what there is to hear and can't see what needs to be seen. Frustration, failure and pain is a constant companion.

The secret...BREAK TRANCE! You must learn to question and question some more. You can not trust what you have been tranced into seeing, hearing, or feeling. Tonight, when you go to sleep, sleep on the other side of the be; sit at a different seat at meal times. For the adventurous, eat with your left hand (or right hand if you are left-handed). Read a book...from the last page; record conversations with those you have the poorest communication with. Look for problem area instead of avoiding them and then come up with three of the most unusual methods for solving the problem. Put a rubber band on your wrist and snap it when ever you feel yourself "dropping out."

Learn to talk to those parts of you that know the difference between trance and what is happening around you. For example, imagine that you begin to feel anxiety. Ask your inner guide to change the feeling into a picture; first a picture of what the feeling itself looks like, and then ask that part to change the picture into one that will help you discover what is really happening for (or to) you. Learn to hear the sound of colors and feelings and to see the feelings and sounds. In short, shake up your systems and break your patterns. (For many interesting and provocative methods of breaking trance, you might even purchase my book, *Monsters and Magical Sticks: There's No Such Thing As Hypnosis*.) Last, but not least, find a good hypnotist who will help you to use hypnosis and trance in order to end your hypnotic trance.

Dr. Israel Regardie
One of the foremost authorities on the
theory and practice of Magick.

"...a representative of the great 'occult tradition' of the late 19th century, whose major names include Madame Blavatsky, W.B. Yeats, MacGregor Mathers, A.E. Waite, Aleister Crowley and Dion Fortune. Even in such distinguished company, Regardie stands out as a figure of central importance."
 –Colin Wilson

THE MIDDLE PILLAR
Dr. Israel Regardie
Chapter 1 from New Falcon Publication:
The Middle Pillar, Third Printing 2022

To me one of the most significant and extraordinary characteristics of modern thought is the widespread circulation of books on psychology in its various branches. There is a general interest in matters dealing with the mind–especially with that aspect of the hinterland of the mind which has been named the Unconscious for want of better words and also because its realm at the moment is so ambiguous to us. There could hardly be an educated individual who has not some slight degree of acquaintance with this analytical psychology. Even if this familiarity ran only to an acquaintance with several of the more commonly employed *cliches*–such as libido, the unconscious, conflicts and resistances, neuroses and complexes–that in itself would be indicative of a phenomenon which surely has occurred seldom before in the history of civilised thought.

To meet this widespread interest in matters psychological, a number of books have been written to give the general reader some notion of that peculiar world with which it is the province of the analyst to deal. Quite a number of these are extremely informative, providing a very sane and balanced view of the subject. On the other hand, as is inevitable, there is a large number which might just as well have remained unwritten. One of the most curious misconceptions promulgated by some of these latter is the fact that analytical psychology—and here I use this term in its widest sense to cover the various schools inaugurated by Freud, Jung, Adler, etc.,—is a thing quite apart, and that the one thing which stamped our ancestors as barbarians and savages was their utter lack of acquaintance with psycho-therapy. It would be totally absurd for anyone to minimise all that has been achieved by modern psychology, due to the efforts of such astute investigators as Freud and Jung. But it is abundantly clear that their protagonists—psychological extremists—go entirely too far in disclaiming the intelligence and insight of our predecessors. For the facts are, as but little research indicates, that so far from being ignorant of analytical psychology, the ancients, and particularly those of the East and hither East, had evolved a highly complex and elaborate scheme not only of analysis, but also of spiritual development and synthesis.

Some orthodox die-hards may question the relationship of modern psychology with discredited oriental and archaic techniques for the unfolding of man's higher or spiritual nature. In practice, however, such a relationship does indubitably exist. It is a fact of clinical and consulting-room experience. For, during the course of a protracted analysis, the cruder and more superficial unconscious levels having been uncovered and moral conflicts resolved, symbols and themmotifs of a religious or spiritual nature do make their entry across the threshold of consciousness. This entry is by way of dream, intuition, and by direct apprehension. Not only is this so, but they exert a potent influence on the entire personality, producing integrity, a new and more equilibrated attitude towards life, and an unification of the various strata of consciousness which collectively we call man.

What modern psychology has quite possibly accomplished is an advance over the efforts of our predecessors in the way of a cathartic technique. Moreover, because of modern devices, the methods of analytical psychology have been brought nearer to the understanding and convenience of the ordinary man of the street. In the past, the techniques of attainment, Mysticism, Magic, and Yoga, or by whatever names of such systems were denoted, were always several removes from the ken of the average individual.

The psychologies of the past may be summarised by the use of the words Yoga and Magic. The subject of Yoga has already been excellently dealt with by several able and competent writers, requiring therefore but little mention here. Such a book as *Yoga and Western Psychology* by Geraldine Coster must certainly take its place historically as a genuine and first-rate contribution to the progress of analytical psychology. There is also the compilation of the Buddhist Lodge *Concentration and Meditation*, a handbook on that subject of great merit. A number of modern psychologists have also examined the subject of Yoga and meditation as a whole, and have found much that is sympathetic to the explanatory of their own systems. And furthermore, the mystical systems posit a goal and a general schema which expand the rather hazy and indeterminate character of a very large part of our psycho-therapeutic systems.

Analytical Psychology and Magic comprise in my estimation two halves or aspects of a single technical system. Just as the body and mind are not two separate units, but are simply and dual manifestations of an interior dynamic "something" so psychology and Magic comprise similarly a single system whose goal is the integration of the human personality. Its aim is to unify the different departments and functions of man's being, to bring into operation those which previously for various reasons were latent. Incidentally, its technique is such that neurotic symptoms which were too insistent upon expression either become eliminated or toned down by a process of equilibration.

It will be obvious, then, that by Magic we are not considering a theatrical craft or jugglery–and certainly not that mediaeval superstition which was the child of ignorance begotten by fear and terror. These definitions should be expunged from our thinking. For centuries Magic has been quite erroneously associated with such pathologies as witchcraft and demonolatry due to the duplicity of charlatans and the reticence of its own so-called authorities. Even today, the custodians of knowledge, harassed by personal problems and more especially by their own power complex are still adamant in their traditional refusal to circulate a more accurate description of the nature of Magic. Possibly even they have lost all understanding of its principles. No wonder is it that misconception exists. With the exception of very few works which have attracted the attention of but a fractional part of the reading public, little has been written to act as a definitive exposition of what Magic really is. Inasmuch as something of the nature of modern Psychology is at least partially understood by a fair section of the educated world, were it said that Magic is akin to and concerns itself with that same subjective realm of psychology, some notion of its character and objectives come within hailing distance.

So far as the average man or aspirant to Magic is concerned, unquestionably the analytic technique should comprise the first stage of the routine employed in spiritual development. For until one understands himself according to that peculiarly penetrating light which Psychology has thrown upon our motives, he cannot hope to bring effectively into operation the dormant side of his nature. And lest anyone casually dismiss this desirable self-knowledge as a goal easily attained to or, it may be, already obtained, one can only utter a solemn warning that this is not so simple as at first sight seems. That self-knowledge is necessary to the pursuit of Magic is self-evident. At once we are faced at the portal by guardians armed to the teeth. Such queries confront us as: suppose the interest in spiritual culture were motivated by a desire to escape from the turbulence of physical life? What if one's stubbornly defended point of view were only an elaborate rationalisation to conceal the sense of insecurity, the dull but insistent ache of inferiority? These are quite often the unrecognised factors which compel refuge in the religious avocation–even in various branches of science too. The search for, and quite often assumed discovery of some paternal-like god or a testy senior after the fashion of Jehovah, frequently has its origins in an adolescent rejection of the father. This, deliberately forgotten, has become so deep, that the inner psychic necessity for the authority and affection of the father is unconsciously projected outwards into a terrifying and awe-inspiring deity. Discernment of the true motives of conduct and attitude towards life is, therefore, an absolute essential. This accomplished, then may be examined that other side of the medallion which is man's own psyche.

As a practical system, Magic is concerned not so much with analysis as with bringing into operation the creative and intuitive parts of man. A psychological technique can never be a wholly integrative one until it accepts this spiritual side of man and assists the analysand in the recognition of or acquaintance with its activity. At this moment, the treatment of these matters remains almost entirely within the domain of Magic alone. Fully does it recognise the necessity for integration. Not only does it accept and recommend the results of analysis, but it proceeds still further. If analysis aims at the acceptance of the Unconscious, and the validity of its coexistence with consciousness, then Magic may be said to be a technique for realising the deeper levels of the Unconscious. These are levels of power and realisation whose value we can but dimly grasp through contemplation of religious figures of the past. Buddha, Jesus, Krishna, St. Francis, and a host of others are instances of such illuminated men–individuals who have striven, all in different ways, to know themselves and attain to a realisation of their true divine nature. If so we wish to learn the techniques they employed, they are identical in spirit call devotion, meditation, and contemplation. They are fundamentally similar with what we now propose to discuss as Magic. In the latter, however, the entire process of attainment has been systematised and developed almost into an exact science, having as its foundation the discovery of Godhead. While there may be very few in life who can attain to the full realisation of their divine origin and nature, yet for all of us there is some value in Magic, some degree of fulfillment or attainment available. There is none so small as cannot employ it to some good and noble end. None so great as cannot better himself morally and otherwise, thus rendering himself more efficient to cope with and understand life and the world both about and within him. These are objectives which, notwithstanding the magnitudes of their vision, are within the reach of every man.

§

It is not yet the moment to enter into a disquisition on the intricacies of magical ritual. But in order to expound fundamental psychological and spiritual principles it is necessary to refer to what are known technically as the Two Pillars. Halfway between the East and West, and North and South, in a properly instituted Temple are placed two upright pillars. One of these is coloured white, the other black. These pieces of lodge furniture are emblematical of the two opposites functioning in the diverse operations of nature. Just as the Temple represents in miniature the whole of life by which we may ever be confronted, or, rather, the manifold parts of our own inner nature, so these two pillars symbolise some aspect of these phenomena. They represent light and darkness, heat and cold. In man, they stand for love and hate, joy and pain, mind and emotion, life and death, sleeping and waking. Every pair of opposites conceivable to the human mind find their representation in the implication of these two pillars.

Now one of the most important ideas communicated to the student of Magic, in his ceremonial initiation when he is led from one station to another, is that an extreme leaning either to one or the other of the opposites is a very dangerous thing. It is unwise to swing to opposite poles of life's pendulum. "Unbalanced power is the ebbing away of life. Unbalanced mercy is but weakness and the fading out of the will. Unbalanced severity is cruelty and the barrenness of mind." Were we to change the terminology of the speech, instead of the word 'mercy' we might substitute 'emotion', or 'generosity' or 'love'; for 'severity' we may substitute 'power', 'the rational side of us', or 'justice' or 'tyranny'. Either of these qualities when carried to an extreme, unmodified by the other, is conducive to an unhealthy state of psyche. Thus it is, that in so religiously authoritative a book as the Bhagavad-Gita, which some consider one of the finest pieces of devotional and philosophical literature yet penned, we find it stated "Be free from the pairs of opposites."

The whole of life–it is in fact the law of Nature itself– seems to be dominated by these extremes or opposites. "Two contending forces and one which unites them eternally. Two basal angles of the triangle and one which forms the apex. Such is the origin of creation; it is the Triad of Life." Only a little reflection will convince the reader of the truth of this theorem. Until we have acquired wisdom and understanding, we swing during the seventy year span of our lives between self-esteem and self-disgust, from an exaggerated estimation of our fellows to their utter and final condemnation. Age, it is true, does bring moderation and temperance with it. But were this more balanced attitude towards life cultivated, taught or adopted earlier or before middle age set in, how much more efficient could we not be, and what could we not achieve? The technique under consideration consists primarily in the conscious reconciliation of opposing forces. It is this which has been called the development of the Golden Flower.

Before proceeding further, it is a very interesting piece of speculation to consider the trinities of various religions. Most of them resolve themselves when all theological argument and intellectual quibbling are eliminated, into some such relationship as Father, Mother and Son. Osiris, Isis and Horus are an excellent example. This is true also of the Christian system where, upon careful consideration we find the Holy Ghost defined as a feminine aspect of godhead. And in the Hebrew Qabalah we have the Trinity on the Tree of Life of CHESED Mercy, GEVURAH Might and TIPHARAS Equilibrium or Beauty. Co-relating this latter triad with traditional symbolism, CHESED is masculine, referred to Jupiter, as a paternal wisdom symbol. GEVURAH, feminine, is attributed to Mars, indicative of great power. One alchemical aphorism expresses this duality in the words "Man is peace and woman is power." Bearing all these in mind, we conclude that as CHESED represents the Father and GEVURAH the Mother, so TIPHARAS which is Beauty, is the reconciler between them. Interestingly enough, TIPHARAS is referred to the Sun, and corresponds to the third member of the theological trinity, the Son.

Looking at these trinities as so many expressions of psychological fact–that is, as previously defined, as factors active within the psyche itself–we are struck by the similarity of the religious point of view with the idea of the Middle Way. It is the pursuit of this middle path which leads to self-conquest and the steady growth of the Golden Flower, the wakening of the imprisoned soul within.

The Father and Mother may be said to correspond to the two Pillars of the Temple, to the two extremes or opposites. In this sense they are the tendencies exhibited by all the phenomena of Nature. They are the extremes of spirit and matter, love and hate, life and death, ebb and flow, systole and diastole. Nature itself is the embodiment of the two extremes, the two opposites of the Trinity. Man, unenlightened man, one in whom neither wisdom nor understanding has been brought to birth, likewise fashions his life in the way of these two extremes. Or rather, these extremes fashion his life for him. For he is, as though by compulsion, driven by some external force he knows not of, between the poles of extreme love and hate, swinging from kindness and maudlin generosity to bursts of uncontrolled anger, hate and meanness. His actions, almost without a single exception, are so many semi-hysterical flights from pole to pole of his emotions. He is, as it were, under the dominion of the Father and the Mother.

To the student of the psyche, to the one who seeks wisdom and the knowledge of his higher Self, the counsel has always been given to avoid the opposites. His task is to refrain from the compulsion of extreme actions.

In certain schools of Magic, where the rites of initiation were celebrated by Adepts who at one time thoroughly understood the technique they employed, initiation ceremonies depicted the burial of the higher Self and its rebirth by means of a technical system of Magic and Meditation. Therein, the higher Self was always represented by some sacred figure of the major religions–a man who was nearly always shown as the Son of God. The essence of the ethical injunctions of these systems was to develop the Son within. "Unless Christ be born in you…" "Look within; thou are Buddha." I do not believe these images could possibly have reference to any historical individual we know of. But rather I surmise these refer to the gradual bringing into conscious operation of a spiritual point of view, of an equilibrated attitude towards life, an attitude not exclusively directed to any extreme. Recognising the polarity of life, such a point of view sought to steer a middle way between the tortuous and extreme activity of Nature. It is the way of the Reconciler, of keeping to the path between the two Pillars, that balanced and harmonious position in which the candidates of the ancient initiation systems found themselves at the major crisis and climax of their initiation. This is the technique of bringing to birth the golden Sun of TIPHARAS, the Sun of beauty and harmony who is the third person of the trinity. Thus it is that one system nowadays conceives of the Great Work as partaking of the recognition of the Crowned and Conquering Child Horus–he who, while partaking necessarily of the nature of both the Father and the Mother, is simultaneously an entirely different and unique being. Through the result of the union of opposing forces, his nature tends to a new viewpoint in the conquest of life. For the Father and Mother are "those forces whose reconciliation is the key of life."

To illustrate in another way the import of this concept, let us describe it from a practical and physical point of view. One of the major inconveniences which afflicts a large portion of mankind is constipation. In many instances of this disorder, no organic disturbance exists at all; the trouble being principally a functional one. (Though it must be here interpolated that even if it were organic, there is sufficient psychological evidence to indicate that this likewise may ensue from an identical series of causes.) Very often, this malady does not respond to any kind of medical treatment. It is not uncommon for patients to testify that they have been recommended massage, surgical operations, drugs, nature cures and all the other types of cures. In spite of these the illness persists unchanged. Enquiry elicits that there is, frequently, a conscious conflict between two courses of conduct. More often than not, however, the real seat of the conflict is not in consciousness at all, but exists in a far deeper level of mind, in the Unconscious. It was probably around puberty that an already existent conflict developed such acuteness and severity as to require for the psychic safety of the ego to be repressed completely out of sight.

From this, we might conclude–and there is some psychological evidence to this end–that the conflict is one between the instincts and social dictates. That is, because of parental training there is a blind refusal to recognise the necessity for the proper and legitimate expression of the instincts. It is a denial of one side of the personality, a denial without justification or reason. It is as though, while admiring the beauty and form of the lotus, we wished not to be reminded of the slimy source where grow the roots of the plant, and therefore cut the stalk right through, severing the flower from its necessary root. This cutting of the lotus stalk has its counterpart in human minds, many of us having been cut off from our roots. For this denial of the instinctual life, in which the conscious existence after all has its roots, and this persistent repression, cause some degree of dissociation. That is, a severance of the integrity and unity of the psyche. The psychosis, if sufficiently intense or prolonged, produces symptoms of various sorts ranging from lack of vitality, irritability, constipation, and a host of other physical and nervous disorders.

With such a problem, there is but one logical method of attack. It is to recognise quite clearly that the physical symptoms are the results of an internal conflict, a conflict between the needs of the body and the self-sufficiency or cowardice of the mind. It is a conflict between the necessity to the expression of emotion and feeling, and the imperious urge of the ego to escape from a vulnerable constituent of its nature, that principle which at one time had been susceptible to hurt and injury. With the frank recognition of the conflict, one should endeavor to recollect the events of his early childhood, bringing up as many memories as possible of that period, experiencing neither shame nor remorse at his discoveries. Confronting these memories with the knowledge that as an adult in whom is the light of reason, he understands that his mature mind can dissipate the infantile emotion connected with early experiences, in which shame or inferiority or insecurity was felt. In this way, he links and applies mind to emotion, thus avoiding within him the uncontrolled play of the opposites. Their existence is neither denied nor frustrated. This is a vital point to be understood. No denial or rejection should be countenanced of what manifestly is an actual fact, no stubborn refusal to admit and accept a part of his own nature. As we have seen, the denial of any function of the self leads to dissociation, and the latter results in nervous and physical disorders.

Face the fact that at one time there was a denial of one phase of life, and thus accept the conflict. Accept it, knowing that so long as we remain human, these conflicts are bound to be our lot. In our present stage of evolution, they are part and parcel of human nature, and so cannot be avoided. But what can be eliminated is the ignorant attitude so often adopted towards them. For these opposites, the two Pillars of the Temple, their magical images or prototypes, represent "those eternal forces betwixt which the equilibrium of the universe dependeth. Those forces whose reconciliation is the Key of Life, whose separation is evil and death." This, then is the solution to conflict. They must be reconciled.

Let me recapitulate. There must be the clear recognition of the conflict. Its exact nature must be analysed and faced, and its presence accepted in all its implications.

One must endeavour to bring up into consciousness, so far as the capabilities of the mind permit, all the memories of childhood. In a word, he should attempt to perform a species of what is called in the Buddhist system the *Sammasati* meditation. This consists in a cultivation and rigid examination of memory. The idea involved here is not that these recollections in themselves are worth anything, but that raising them up to the surface releases a great deal of tension associated with early experiences. There is often a typing up of nervous energy in childhood experiences, in trivial events which are allowed to be forgotten and to sink into unconsciousness. But this forgetfulness does not overcome the shock of nervous exhaustion connected with them. On the contrary, they set up what are called resistances–resistances to the flow of life and vitality from the primitive and vital layers of the Unconscious level.

"What matters," remarks Georg Groddeck the brilliant German physician-psychologist, is not to make conscious anything at all of the Unconscious, but to relieve what is imprisoned, and in so doing it is by no means rare for the repressed material to sink into the depths instead of coming into consciousness.... What is decisive in the success of treatment is the removal of resistance."

Beginning with the actual events of the day upon which the reader determines to commence this exercise, the meditation should gradually extend its field of vision until ultimately the events and occurrences of the earliest years are brought into the light of day. The technique is principally one of the training of the mind to think backwards. Difficult though at first it may seem, practice leads the student slowly and gradually to facility in the art of remembering. The facts of memory confronted fearlessly, without shame and discomfiture, the resistance to the flow of vitality between the various levels of consciousness is broken down, restoring physical, nervous and spiritual health.

As the childhood memories are exposed, the student will see for himself in what way the conflict now bothering him came into manifestation. Since by definition a neurosis is a maladaptation of the psyche to life itself, by this process of remembering he will see in what way he failed to respond properly to the phenomena of his existence.

Realising this, and recognising thoroughly the nature of his conflict, he must now endeavour to ignore it. More accurately a more positive attitude should be adopted. He must develop in an entirely new direction. It must be remembered, however, and this is important, that to ignore any symptom of conflict as manifested in mind or body, is dangerous until the conflict in question has been recognised and accepted. The unconditional acceptance almost invariably acts as its resolution. Any other attitude constitutes an escape.

The escape mechanism is that so frequently adopted by the neurotic and must be avoided. It is the way of the coward. To face the conflict is to rob it and its consequences of crippling fear. Honesty with oneself acts as a catharsis. One finds himself endued with a new courage and greater ability to face one's problem in an entirely new and more practicable way. Given the recognition of the conflict causing constipation, the symptom itself may be severely ignored, relying upon the bowel after the lapse of some days to recommence functioning of its own accord. The conflict and the warring between the two sides of the psyche, tied a knot as it were in consciousness preventing the perfect functioning of the whole. The immediate result of this is an impediment in the free movement of nervous energy in the body-mind system, causing stasis in that part of the system having a relationship or correspondence with the factors concerned in the conflict.

Occult theory as we have it from tradition may be extremely useful here. With some degree of practical experience, we could easily discover the precise nature of the original conflict by a consideration of that part of the organism to the symptoms of which our attention is attracted. For example, consider one troubled by nephritis. One of the most significant aspects of the magical tradition is Astrology. In this latter science the kidneys are referred to the operation of the planet Venus. As we know from mythology, Venus is the deity concerned with love, feeling and emotion. We would surmise therefore that in the event that the love or emotional life of an individual has been frustrated or repressed to such a point where the psyche finally refused to continue living whilst hampered by such a neurosis, some expression of that frustration could be transferred to the neighborhood of the kidneys. Were the frustration complete and devastating to the psyche, it is not impossible that we should find a cancer–the symptom *par excellence* of the death-wish, the so-called suicide complex indicative of a division in the psyche's integrity.

Moreover, we could proceed a step further. We might enquire as to whether the affliction were on the right or left, remembering the Qabalistic definition of the Left Pillar as the side of Mercy, and that on the Right as the Pillar of Severity. "Unbalanced mercy is weakness and the fading out of the will. Unbalanced severity is cruelty and the barrenness of mind."

Enquiry might elicit the fact that an afflicted left kidney were symptomatic of one who had been afraid to taste life to the full. Or on the other hand, out of sheer compensation, had lived so completely as to have over-indulged. The right kidney would indicate symptoms of severe and violent repression on principle–where the entire emotional life had been so subjected to continuous frustration because of an ethical standard that the outraged eros reacted upon the body either with acute nephritis or it may be with cancer.

Where there is trouble with the legs, the patient being unable to stand and confined to the bed, some psychological thinkers proffer some such explanation as this. The legs are the things we stand on, that which gives support to the body. In the symbolic pageantry utilised by the Unconscious–and it must be understood that the activity of the Unconscious proceeds almost exclusively through what are to us symbols–

the instinctual life is our mental support. It is that which we tend to rely upon, our stability and foundation, during life. Should therefore our understanding of life fall short of what it should be for us–and obviously that standard varies with different people–so that we unduly repress our instincts to the point when the resulting sense of insecurity and anxiety become intolerable, the psyche achieves a revenge through an affliction of the supports of the personality. Thus it is that we learn, so it is said, by illness. When our supports, no matter of what nature, have been annihilated, we sometimes seek to enquire into causes and origins. When the enquiry is honestly furthered, with a sincere view to self-knowledge, and internal resistance broken down by meditation or analysis, no doubt recovery would ensue. That is to say, the disappearance of the alarming symptoms, and a return of normal function.

The solvent to these difficulties, the practical solution of the problem, consists primarily in the elimination so far as possible of fear. Of course, from the larger point of view, fear is an essential part of our make-up. Man is so puny a creature on the face of the earth, and Nature is vast and terrible in her operations. How else could it be that fear eats at the heart of each of us? But this is a wholesome fear–a fear which is the beginning of wisdom. The emotion under consideration is a pathological thing–fear of the future, fear of position, a needless worrying about affairs which cannot be helped or changed, at least not by hugging a constant fear that they will change in a manner that is painful and sad. From the spiritual point of view, fears such as we have named act as a great freezer, an inhibitor of action and of the free flow of vital energy upon a given course of action because it may lead to failure, or whose apprehension of success and of the future generally, is hardly likely to accomplish very much. "Fear is failure" says one magical aphorism, "and the forerunner of failure. Be thou therefore without fear, for in the heart of the coward, virtue abideth not."

One of the most interesting instances of the psychotherapeutic attitude to fear and anxiety and the escape-problem as a whole was Groddeck's treatment, when he was a physician before applying psychology to his problems, of certain cases of indigestion and nervous dyspepsia. One of the psychological theorems regarding this form of discomfort is that it is due to anxiety. We all know how bad news or worry affects the digestion, from turning the food sour to taking away the appetite. But the root cause of this particular anxiety is not the problem in hand, but the anxiety which has its roots in an early conflict and is made the worse by the occurrence of an immediate problem evoking conflict and anxiety. Groddeck's treatment–almost the homeopathic principle–emphasised or comprised a diet of precisely those foods which formerly disagreed with his patient. If eggs were the cause of indigestion the diet would comprise eggs until eventually the psychic would give up attempting to evade the associations which had been linked to eggs, and the digestive trouble would in time disappear. To force the psyche to face its problems and accept them was his idea rather than that the psyche should continually baulk from and attempt to flee the symptoms it threw up in the body. The unconditional acceptance of the conflict, and the associations connected with it, was the first step towards cure. The technique is, in a word or two, an attack on the escape mechanism. Integrity cannot be won by an escapist attitude towards life. The reward of the attitude which escapes from problems and the reality of life is more likely than not to be nothing but the gnawing pain of guilt and sin.

The same method is often made use of in other forms of therapy. Amongst these, for example, is the treatment of nightmares by analysis. The terror experienced in nightmare, causing the dreamer to awaken bathed in perspiration, angered by a palpitation of the heart, and experiencing an inexplicable sense of impending catastrophe, is likewise due to some conflict or other. Its nature, being unconscious, can only be determined by the context of the dream, and by the lengthy process of confession, free association, and reductive analysis.

But if the dreamer can be trained in his waking state to realise that the nightmare is only the expression of an internal conflict, then he has proceeded halfway to the point where it will cease to bother him. He must accept the presence of such a disorder rather than attempt to escape it, because escape is not an adequate solution of a psychic problem.

This discovery was brought home to us during the war. Amongst the soldiers at the front were those who would not recognise the very obvious fact, that war was a dangerous matter and that they were afraid. This they would not accept, though underneath a veritable torrent of fear was raging, and the whole of the instinctive impulse was to bolt from the scene of battle. Those who recognised this impulse but at the same time saw that flight was impossible and that the war had to be seen through, came to no mental or spiritual harm. It was the former type, suffering from a terrible fear but boasting that they were not in the least afraid, who became affected by shell-shock. Shell-shock–the shock experienced by the nervous system through the devastating noise of explosion, had nothing to do with their actual trouble at all. The cause was simply a cowardly refusal to face the conflict raging in the psyche. And when this became so intolerable, an actual split occurred in consciousness, so that there was a gap in memory, awareness and in efficiency.

With the acceptance of the theory of conflict as a cause of nightmare, a subtle change gradually creeps into the nightmare-dream. The following is one rather fine example, together with the method of dealing with it.

A woman patient frequently dreamed that she was hanging from a rope in a room which had an enormously high ceiling, about fifty or sixty feet high. The rope was affixed by a hook to the ceiling, and the weight imposed upon the hook was gradually loosening the plaster around. Any moment, the hook would tear loose from the ceiling, and the body would be dashed to the ground. At this juncture of the dream, unable to face the terror of being hurled to death on the ground, the woman awoke in a frenzy of fear, screaming. The advice given in this particular case–and since the dream is a typical nightmare, the same technique may be widely recommended–was to suggest to the woman the advisability of meditating on the dream before falling to sleep at night. The suggestion was to lengthen the term of the dream so as to invite the nightmare and observe what happened when the plaster did finally break, tearing the hook from the ceiling.

Constant and deep reflection on the dream's theme before sleep was the method by which the Unconscious could so be influenced as to induce a vigilant attitude even during the progress of the phantasy. The topic of meditation would also be the conscious application of the idea of non-resistance. Let the catastrophe occur, and see what happens. If the phantasy is being perched on a high cliff and at any moment there is a danger of being hurled to the ground, awaking at mid-point in a sweat of fear, then gradually train the mind to thrust out all resistance to the fall. By methods such as these resistance and repression is broken down and fear eliminated from the sphere of consciousness.

Here, some word should be said about repression and the means of its elimination. A great many people have come to believe, through a very casual reading of some of the early psycho-analytic literature, that psychology countenances the removal of repression by means which are unethical and anti-social. Nothing could be further from the truth. Repression is always defined as an unconscious and automatic process. It is a process by which the personality protects itself against distasteful concepts, by thrusting them without the horizon of consciousness into the dark and forbidding region of the Unconscious. Since this process begins very early in life, the Unconscious is by middle age stuffed with a mass of repressed material–ideas about parents and relatives, associations connected with environment, infantile beliefs and actions. Suppression, on the other hand, is a deliberate and conscious thing. It presupposes a process of conscious selection and elimination, in which one alternative is suppressed in favour of another.

It is repression, the unconscious process of thrusting things out of sight, which is the dangerous method. It is dangerous because repressed emotions and feelings lock up memory and power in the Unconscious. Because ideas become associated with each other, forming definite complexes, there is, if repressed memories begin to grow by association, a splitting off of one side of the mind at the expense of the other with a consequent locking up of energy and vitality which should be available for the entire personality. The conquest of repression proceeds as with the conquest of internal conflict previously described.

There is no need to live an anti-social or vicious life, one of self-indulgence or of degradation as so many people think. To be free from a repression does not argue that one should have behaved like "a young man about town." Though that is not to say that a reasonable satisfaction of the instinctual life should be eschewed where this is at all possible. But the frank realisation and acceptance of the human personality as many-sided, and a refusal to blind oneself to experience no matter of what kind, will go far towards relieving the partition erected between the Unconscious and the Conscious, and removing resistance and repression.

To restate the attitude expounded in this chapter, I conceive of analytical psychology as the spouse of the ancient system of Magic. For psychology has succeeded in evolving a system which can be applied to almost any individual who wishes to know the several departments and constituents of his own personality. Possibly for the first time in the history of civilised thought, there is a technique which is of inestimable value to the average man. It is of supreme value to the student of Magic and Mysticism, who, too often, labours under several delusions of what it is that he hopes to accomplish, and in what length of time he will do so. A study of analysis will prove first of all that he cannot proceed quicker than his own Unconscious permits him. This will prevent gate-crashing, and an irrational enthusiasm and desire for speed. Secondly, through the elimination of erroneous ideas as to himself, the phantasms of wish-fulfilment and insensate day-dreaming, he will have obtained more comprehensive account of what magical and meditation systems can accomplish, can what degree of achievement in these spheres is open to him. He will be entirely less subject to delusion and deception because his attraction to Magic will not have been caused by the unconscious desire to escape from the pressing problems of his immediate existence with which he finds himself unable efficiently to cope.

Moreover, he will have familiarised himself with the true extent of his own sense of inferiority. The compulsive necessity of becoming unduly aggressive because of an imagined or pathological inferiority will no longer urge him to an intolerable sense of deficiency. Being acquainted with the fundamental problem of insecurity which every thinking individual is bound to have, since man is so apparently insignificant and unimportant when compared to the vastness of the universe, he will not be liable to adopt extreme religious or scientific notions from so-called spiritual experience or laboratory experiment to buttress up his own desire for some one thing which is secure and reliable.

Analysis is the logical precursor of spiritual attainment and magical experiment. It should comprise definitely the first stage of spiritual training. Were it possible, and were there magical schools in existence, it would gratify me enormously to see magical training preceded by six or twelve months of application to reductive analysis, pursued by sympathetic physicians or lay-analysts who had long and intimate experience with clinical work. The magical schools must open a Department of Analytical Psychology, if their own systems are to attain public prominence worthy of attention and patronage. Such schools, though offering courses of training considerably prolonged, would eventually develop such a type of individual that the public would eliminate "dangerous" from its association with Magic, and be obliged to take cognisance of the soundness of its technique. This union of two systems would, for Magic at any rate, build up psychological credit, and a sense of great reliability and prestige would accrue to it.

One of the greatest obstacles to success in Magic, to any kind of worth-while result in the mystical sciences, is that the psycho-emotional system of its average student is hopelessly clogged with infantile and adolescent predilection which have not been recognised as such. The ego is compelled to extreme courses of action, as though by compulsion. And underneath his every activity lurks the unconscious spectre–fear. It is precisely with these monsters of phantasy that analytical psychology can deal effectively, and it is from such absurd obstacles that the magical student is a confirmed but unconscious sufferer.

By associating Magic with analysis, we should be able to avoid the pitfalls into which our predecessors fell so headlong. The production of genius–more specifically a religious and mystical type of genius–ever the goal of Magic, should be more within our grasp than ever before, and considerably more open to achievement.

These ideas are mentioned not because a systematic union of Magic and Psychology will be here presented, but in the hope that this effort will spur some psychologist acquainted with magical and mystical techniques to attempt such a task. Whoever does succeed in welding the two indissolubly together, to him mankind will ever be grateful. For such a union comprises the marriage of the archaic with the modern, the Unconscious with the Conscious–the precursor of the birth of the Golden Flower not for any individual alone but for mankind as a whole.

Dr. Israel Regardie (1907-1985) was an Adept of the Hermetic Order of the Golden Dawn and one of the greatest exponents of the Western Esoteric Tradition of the 20th century. He is known as one of the leading authorities on the theory and practice of Magick. In addition to his extensive writings, Regardie practiced as a chiropractor and as a neo-Reichian therapist.

New Falcon Publications
Publisher of Controversial Books and CDs
Invites You to Visit Our Website:
http://www.newfalcon.com

At the Falcon website you can:

- Browse the online catalog of all our great titles, including books by Robert Anton Wilson, Christopher S. Hyatt, Israel Regardie, Aleister Crowley, Timothy Leary, Osho, Lon Milo DuQuette and many more
- Find out what's available and what's out of stock
- Get special discounts
- Order our titles through our secure online server
- Find products not available anywhere else including:
    - One of a kind and limited availability products
    - Special packages
    - Special pricing
- And much, much more

Get online today at http://www.newfalcon.com